Walking in Humble Spirit

Jenny Lee

and

Michael Cormier

GREYMERE

Cover art © 2017 by Jeremiah Taggert
Tigertyphoon4711@gmail.com

ISBN-13: 978-1979656979
ISBN-10: 1979656975

Questions and comments may be directed to the author at
http://www.jennyssight.net

To my father, Johnny S. Dennis,
and my grandmother, Lela Flynn

You pursued your life fearlessly,
and your influence was enormous

– Jenny

WALKING IN HUMBLE SPIRIT

Foreword

We humans are insatiably curious.

It's one of the things that drive our progress. From the time we first became self-aware, we wondered who we were and how we got here. At the same time, we sought to understand the environment surrounding us.

Eventually, our questions expanded and we wondered about our earthly home as a whole. Some of our conclusions seemed obvious, but turned out to be dead wrong. For example, we were once absolutely certain that the Earth was flat and that you would fall off the edge if you sailed out on the ocean too far. To think otherwise was just foolish! Then some brave people tested the theory that the Earth was not flat at all, but round. Thankfully (for them), they were right.

We also looked to the sky and drew conclusions about celestial bodies. Noting the sun's movement across the heavens, the question naturally came about: does the sun revolve around the Earth, or does the Earth revolve around the sun? For centuries, we believed the sun revolved around us. Religious doctrine even commanded it. Then Copernicus and Galileo risked everything by theorizing, then proving, that the opposite was true.

As for the rest of the universe, scientists are still learning wondrous things once thought impossible. Two decades ago—a fraction of a second in human history—we finally answered a question that had fascinated scientists ever since Galileo: are there other planets beyond our solar system? Only since 1992 have we had a definitive answer to this question. Today, we take for granted that there are probably billions of exoplanets. Lately, we've come to understand that many of these planets may be very much like Earth. The potential significance is mindboggling.

From relativity to quantum mechanics, dark matter to dark energy, every generation has contributed something to a general understanding of who we are, what we are and where we live. This generation and the next will take for granted things we can only imagine today. And perhaps the most important understanding will be the way all physical things relate to the non-physical realm.

Leading the way will be people like Jenny Lee.

Every now and then someone comes along who, seemingly with no particular reason, draws a little more light than others. Jenny is one of those people. Born with unusual inner vision and spiritual connection, Jenny, like so many others possessing what is sometimes loosely termed "the gift," was discouraged as a child from revealing what she knew and saw. Family, teachers, clergy—everyone made her feel her gift wasn't really a gift at all, but a "condition," and a bad one. That it indicated some kind of disturbed mind or evil influence. In the era in which Jenny grew up this "condition" was commonly misunderstood the same way other "conditions" were misunderstood throughout history, as the witch hunts and the Inquisition bear witness. And yet, like others before her, Jenny could not ignore her ability. It was only when she accepted it, and even embraced it, that she found a kind of inner peace most of us never experience. She felt herself connect to something larger, something universal. A spiritual door opened. When she discovered that her ability could help others, there was no going back.

This story of progress and enlightenment isn't unique. You may have read about similar journeys before. What *is* unique is how Jenny does it, the way she channels and gathers information. Even more important is the way she lives her flesh-bound life within a universal context, such that the spiritual aspect of life naturally permeates everything she does and everything that happens to her.

And here's the best news of all: everyone can live such a joyful, universally connected existence.

Jenny's ability isn't exclusive; it's something most of us can tap into, at least to some extent. For most people this ability will remain nascent all their lives, but it's still there. We all have spirit guides waiting to help and protect us; we just need to acknowledge them and include them in our lives. That's what this book is all about.

The time is ripe to become more spiritual. In this new millennium we are making great strides in discovering who we are in the context of the rest of the universe. It's a time of human progression, of *personal* progression. That progression must naturally include complete spirituality. Someday, we will take this aspect of our existence for granted, just like we now take for granted that the Earth is round and that it revolves around the sun.

Ever since Jenny began helping others with her readings, remote viewings and healings many years ago, she's been asked by countless people when she might write a book to help others learn what she knows. This is that book. This is Jenny's gift of enlightenment for all those seekers who are ready to let their own spiritual connection develop and blossom.

So open all the windows and doors of your mind and get ready for a new perspective to waft in on a new and fresh breeze. A breeze that was always there, though beyond the reach of everyday senses. Strain your inner ear and listen to the sound that's carried on that breeze. You will hear the first faint notes of a song that at first seems unfamiliar. But it's getting louder, and soon you will hear it even better, until the first faint glimmer of recognition comes to you . . .

Then embrace your future.

Michael Cormier

Introduction

Just as a candle cannot burn without fire, men cannot live without a spiritual life – Buddha

My name is Jenny Lee, and I'm a psychic medium. Not by job title or training, but by design—though not my own design.

As you get started on this book, and the spiritual journey I hope it encourages you to take, I want to make one thing very clear: I'm very much like you. In fact, about ninety-nine percent of me resembles every person on earth. My basic needs are pretty much the same: food, shelter, companionship, love, hope. Faith, too. We all need faith, whether we care to admit it or not. It's hardwired into each and every one of us, same as the rest of our basic needs. There's a good reason, too, but I'll get back to that soon enough.

What's important to understand is that I'm like you, which of course means you are like me. You should keep this in mind as you turn the pages that follow. No matter who you are, *you are like me*. The only difference is that I've had the great fortune to experience things most of you have not. Yet, contrary to what some people may think, this does not make me special. Why? Because what I experience was not meant for only me to experience, and what I know was not meant for only me to know. Most of you are capable of developing this same inner sight. I would compare it to a child born with a physical deficiency that can be overcome, such as underdeveloped muscles. With the right therapy, that child will soon be out there with the rest of the children, running around the playground and even excelling at sports.

But make no mistake: I do recognize that being born with this ability of mine is a great advantage. Some call it a gift and in a way it really is, with one exception: unlike other gifts, even though I know where it came from I don't know why I was chosen to receive it. I can only guess, but it's really not that important. What matters is that I was bestowed this ability with the expectation that I would use it to help others. For many years I have done this through readings, healings and remote viewing. And now I know there's something else I've been called upon to do: teach.

That's the purpose of this book, to teach. To pass on the knowledge and skills I've spent all of my life learning and developing. For many years I have changed the lives of people through what I'm able to do, yet it did not always change *them*. What I mean is that I gave people information, and in this way I was able to affect their beliefs and give them hope—and yes, faith—which enriched their lives. Unfortunately, however, I did not affect their own innate ability to find truth and balance. People kept coming back to me, grateful for what I had already done for them and eager for more. I was always happy to help, but I always knew it would be temporary and that they were missing out on the deeper benefits of doing it for their selves. Thus, after forty-eight years living side by side with angels and spirit guides, and taking it for granted the way others take breathing for granted, I now know there's another step I'm obligated to take. And that's to teach others how to find the angels and spirit guides that so earnestly want to help them take charge of their own lives.

What you are about to read *will* change your life. It will answer many of the questions you've asked yourself since your earliest days in Sunday school and science class: Is there a God, and what does he want from us? What is his plan? Why are we here, and where do we go after we die? What is out there, out beyond our planet, our solar system, our galaxy, and why is it even there? We humans can't know everything; we weren't designed for that. Yet it's been theorized that we use only about ten percent of our brains. I'm not sure that's accurate, but I do know we use only a fraction of our *minds*. Imagine what we could know and do if we plugged into the rest? I'm only asking you to tap into a small fraction; a portion that is in perfect working order yet presently lies dormant. In there you will find knowledge that we all have, but which we shelved and forgot about centuries ago. That knowledge is there in you. Right now. And I'm going to show you how to reach it. It may be tucked away on the highest shelf and you may have to get on your tiptoes and stretch, but you *can* reach it. When you do, you'll discover a place you were always meant to go, populated by friends you've craved since childhood. Friends who will never let you down, so long as you're willing to listen.

Now, for those of you who are still skeptical, I say this: you opened this book for a reason. No one forced you (we should hope!). You are reading these words because you wanted to know something. Maybe you thought you were just curious, but that would be an oversimplification. In the foreword to this book, mention was made of the overbearing curiosity of human beings. Yes we are driven to know, but not just for the sake of knowing. We're all on a journey of self-discovery, a journey that began a very long time ago and which fell dormant after the age of empirical science kicked in. By then we had developed organized religion and all the dogma and ritual that goes with it in order to satisfy our need to know our place in the universe. This was somewhat useful, and it got us through many centuries. Yet it did not go far enough. For one thing, it did not adequately explain our role in the larger scheme of things. Interestingly, the cultures that came closest were considered to be primitive, and yet it turns out they had more on the ball than the rest of us! They at least sought an understanding of mankind's place in the universe, how we relate to all things physical and non-physical, seen and unseen.

Ironically, perhaps, it has taken all these centuries of devotion to science to finally come around to a more spiritual definition of the universe. The more scientists explore the physical universe, discovering marvels they never expected—some of which they never even thought possible—the more they're beginning to awaken to just how deeply connected we humans are to all things. What's more, scientists have finally begun to acknowledge that science and spiritualism might not be so separate after all. I personally leave the physical part to them to figure out; the realm I work in every day is the spiritual. Not in theory, as a minister or rabbi or other spiritual leader would, but in working application.

That's where the new frontier lies: applied spiritualism. And that's where I want to take you. So if you're ready then turn the page and let's get started.

1.

Who Am I?

If a man does not keep pace with his companions, perhaps it is because he hears a different drummer. Let him step to the music which he hears, however measured or far away. – Henry David Thoreau

We all ask the question from time to time, "Who am I?" Some of us ask it daily. We want to know ourselves: where and who we came from, what we're made of. Even more, we want to understand our true personality. What makes us tick. How we, as individuals, differ from everyone else. Our unique place in the big picture.

Believe it or not, there was a time when "Who am I?" was rarely if ever asked. Certainly our grandparents never did, at least out loud. Yet it was always implied, wasn't it? Every time they made a choice about a career (assuming there was a choice to be had!), or marital partner, their decision spoke volumes about whom they were. The way they worshipped, their philosophy about such things as child rearing, how they responded to adversity – these were clues as well. What our great-grandparents didn't have the freedom to do is evaluate their personal place in the larger scheme. Instead, they were simply taught there was a right way and a wrong way to live your life. You made a decision between the two, and that was about all the choice you got.

As for me, I never had to ponder who I was because I was shown right from the beginning. Most of you, on the other hand, were not. Still, you have the ability not only to know what your society says you are, but what it doesn't— and can't. Not just on a surface level—tastes, interests, goals and all the rest—but your place in the universal picture.

As I said, I learned this early on. So early, in fact, that it was permanently imprinted on my soul from birth. I did not choose who I am or what I'm able to do. It was bestowed for reasons not entirely clear to me even to this day. Not that my birth or my circumstances were anything remarkable. I was born into an average family in the late sixties. My father was an auto mechanic, my mother a nurse's aide. We lived in the Colfax section of Denver, a rough part of town back then, and we didn't have a lot of money so we made do in a small rented house. I had an older sister and brother and two younger brothers, so I was smack-dab in the middle where kids usually go unnoticed. But believe me I did not go unnoticed.

While still in my mother's womb I began to experience angels and spirits. These came through as a distinct vibration. Whenever I speak of vibrations in this book I'm referring to the frequencies or tones that some people sense, and which move them spiritually. Vibrations are what make the universe tick. Everything—organic or mineral—is constantly exposed to different vibrations and gives off vibrations of their own. For me, it was always like listening to a sound wave of information coming across like a radio signal. Only it came from within. Once I tuned in I stayed with it, and I've been tuning in ever since.

The reason I paid attention early on was that the vibration felt familiar to my soul, like I had known it all along, maybe from a previous existence. I knew I was meant to stay on this wavelength and never deviate from it. And as I said, I was already aware of this vibration at birth and it had stayed with me. I knew my soul had come to me from somewhere else and was planted in my physical body, as though I'd been assigned a mission.

If you already guessed that my unswerving devotion to certain vibrations and the information they gave me was going to cause problems as I grew up, you're right. Yet I refused to live my life any other way. I realized that the communication I had tuned into was more reliable than any information I received from flesh-and-blood dwellers on this earth, and therefore had to take priority. This included all the information handed out by my parents and teachers, and all other authority figures. But don't misunderstand me. It wasn't that living people had nothing useful to teach me. Like any other child, I welcomed what I learned from everyday interaction with my community and my environment. Yet not all of it was useful, or even accurate. Much of it was dishonest or based on prejudice, ignorance or plain error, whereas the vibrations I heard and felt internally never failed me.

So the vibration I received from humans simply became a secondary source to the vibrations I knew internally. Often, it was like getting advice from two sources, and I always went with what I knew was the soundest advice. This higher vibration was grooming me, raising me as it were. I felt like I knew it and it knew me. And I came to trust it implicitly. As you might expect, this became a never-ending source of frustration to adult authority figures, but I didn't care. I went with the advice I trusted most, and quite honestly, it never let me down.

My seemingly stubborn refusal to listen caused other concerns for the adults in my life. Even as a preschool child,

I was always running away. Not exactly the kind of running away we all picture; just moving away from the vibration I didn't need and toward the one that called to me, you might say. I would wander off to other parts of the neighborhood in response to what I was hearing. Yet what I heard wasn't exactly clear at that early stage. I was always searching for something, but never seemed to find it. I would show up at a neighbor's house, and they would take me in safely off the street and feed me and even dress me if I wasn't dressed appropriately. Meanwhile, my mother would be having a fit wondering where I was. She always tried to keep me from straying, but it was useless. The energy drawing me away was just too strong.

I was never interested in other kids, only adults. Kids didn't offer much, but I sensed some adults did, so I felt compelled to seek them out. I was searching for something familiar. A familiar soul, perhaps. Sometimes I thought I was getting close, but I was always disappointed. Still, I knew there was someone out there I could identify with, someone with the right vibration, and I needed to find that person.

But I never really did—not in my younger years, anyway—and so I kept my thoughts and feelings to myself. This was probably a good thing. If I had spoken up at that point I'm sure it would have stirred up a lot of controversy, and I would have found myself being poked and prodded and asked a lot of questions by physicians and psychiatrists. It did come out in my actions, though. I remember when I was about five my brother and sister accidentally set the garage behind our house on fire. As everyone else ran, I calmly got out the garden hose, and while my mother watched in horror, I stood in front of the building spraying it down. I didn't feel any fear because I knew I wouldn't get hurt. My spirit guides had told me I would be okay, and I trusted them.

By then I had begun to understand what these spirit guides were and how they communicated, yet they were by no means the only ones with whom I communicated. Earthbound spirits—souls that had once existed in the flesh and had since died, yet hadn't moved on to the next realm for whatever reason—had begun to seek me out. This especially occurred right after someone passed on. Often, the communication was through one of my dolls. The doll would serve as a sort of conduit: energy would flow through it to me. Dolls can be portals to spirits, and whenever this happened to me it was as if the spirit of the person who'd passed on suddenly discovered a means to communicate with me.

The way I reacted was to bury the doll. It was my way of putting the spirit to rest. I recall burying a doll when I was about five, and my mother caught me doing it. When she asked why, I explained that the girl down the street had died. Mom later learned that a little girl down the street, who we didn't know, had indeed passed away. She'd had some kind of issue with her breathing, Mom told me. But I already knew that.

Another time, I had gone to the emergency room with my mom after cutting my leg. I was being examined when I heard the cries of a young girl of about my own age in a nearby room. All at once I began to feel not only the girl's emotions but also her pain. The pain was all over her body. Somehow I had telepathically tuned into what had happened to the girl and learned that her father had beaten her severely. Though no living person told me, I knew when the girl finally passed on that day because her spirit stayed with me for a while. I buried a doll and the girl crossed over.

As I entered school, my preoccupation with higher vibrations would become something of a problem—at least from the perspective of the adults in my life. In school, if I was allowed to sit still for five minutes with nothing to do I would kind of zone out, paying attention to the spirit guiding me at that particular moment, or even just the environment around me. My teachers couldn't do anything about it. No matter how hard they tried to get me to focus, I would just tune them out. I'm sure this sounds like Attention Deficit Disorder, but that's not what it was at all. It wasn't that I lacked the ability to stay focused. I simply didn't want to. I had begun to feel that what my teachers offered me was not a priority. I was learning from another source, a higher vibration. And lower vibrations mostly annoyed me.

Even in church I found it hard to pay attention. Again, it wasn't that I disrespected what the minister and all the people around me were doing. I just found it boring. Not in the way any other child finds church boring. The information being taught was at a lower vibration, which meant it was useless to me. I had access to higher information through higher vibrations, so why bother? I also sensed that what was being said and done in church was designed for mind control. This isn't to say I'm not spiritual; I'm as spiritual as anyone you'll ever meet. Organized religion just doesn't interest me. Most religious leaders teach things that they don't have a firm grasp of themselves—and those are the ones with *good* intentions. Others are all about mind control and greed and even darker things. Religion can be a very dangerous thing for those who aren't aware.

In my case, I was lucky to be attending church in a mild and relatively harmless environment, yet it just had nothing to offer me. I would be sitting in that church pew, tuned into a spirit that respectfully told me I shouldn't bother listening to the minister, that there was a higher knowledge to be gained elsewhere. Simple as that.

So early on I developed a reputation as a kid who didn't pay attention, who was prone to zoning out. When I wasn't zoning out, my connection to higher knowledge caused me to speak out. Not always with good results, mind you. For instance, when I was about ten, my grandfather died. He had a good soul and I loved him very much. About a year and a half later, my grandmother remarried. I loved grandma, too, and I wanted her to be happy. Yet even at this tender age I could sense this new man in her life was not good. In fact, my spirit guides had told me he didn't really love grandma, that he was a manipulator and only wanted her money. One day, we were visiting at grandma's house and her new husband went to sit down in an old leather recliner that had belonged to my grandfather. I looked very seriously at him and said, "If you sit in that chair you'll die in it." I didn't know why he would die, only that the spirits had told me it would happen. Well, he gave me a strange look — he had no idea how to deal with this comment, especially coming from a ten-year-old—and sat in the chair anyway. Three years later he had a stroke in that chair and died the same day. It was a shock for everyone in the family. Everyone but me.

By that time I was entering a new stage in my development as a sensitive. As my teen years approached, my awareness of other people's energy changed. I felt it in a stronger way, and I did everything to stay away from negative energy. I also started seeing colors. When you look at a person, you probably see only the flesh. Everyone does, at least in the beginning. But when you're tuned in you become sensitive to other things, especially the energy surrounding living matter. It comes across to me in colors. You might think I'm talking about auras; if so, you would be wrong. What I see is similar to what the alien saw in that old sci-fi movie, *Predator*. Another good example is the things Scarlett Johansson saw in the more recent sci-fi movie, *Lucy*. I don't just see the surface flesh and other organic material. I see the energy, the "invisible" things going on all around and even inside this living thing. It's like looking at a radar screen or a temperature gun.

These images come in waves. They also come in symbols like circles, squares, rods and swords. It's like I have some kind of screen in front of my eyes. Sometimes the energy actually comes up close to me. My spirit guides trust me enough to show me these things, knowing I will handle it appropriately. They allow me to see in more depth than the everyday. They decide what I will see, yet they seldom let me or my subjects down, for it's this ability that lies at the core of everything I can do sight-wise. I will explain this more in future chapters.

Getting back to my teen years, it was around this time I began perceiving people much differently. I started really tuning in, but not always with confidence, at least at first. When you're new to something like this, being a flesh-and-blood human, you find yourself doubting what you see. After experiencing it long enough, however, it's like anything else you do in repetition. You begin to trust it, just like an experienced concert pianist trusts his body and brain to produce flawless music without even thinking. And the more you trust, the stronger your ability becomes.

So the soul is in charge of all physical functions, definitely more so than the flesh. As you expect more from that realm and trust it more, your abilities develop. You start to see more, as I did. As a teenager I saw colors in people, yet for each individual person the colors meant something different. The spirits, through telepathy, told me what they meant. Hence, I would "see" with my mind's eye things that no one else knew existed, even within themselves, like illnesses and disease. I could smell and taste things, too, and I often pinpointed the region. Yet I couldn't pinpoint the exact organ. For some reason, to this day I've never developed that exact accuracy.

But my abilities developed in other ways as my teen years came on. In so many ways, in fact, that it strained just about all of my relationships. My teachers had just about given up on me, and so had the other kids at school. My mom didn't know what to do with me, either. She tried the usual methods to get me to pay attention and toe the line, but nothing worked. Not discipline, not harsh words, not warnings. How was any of this going to stop me from paying attention to a higher vibration that I trusted more than anything else? Finally, she took me to a psychiatrist. He did his best; I'll give him that. But everything he talked about fell on deaf ears, or rather ears that were tuned in elsewhere. When it came time for him to ask me if I had anything to say, my answer was a polite, but flat, "No." I was only reacting to what the spirits told me to say. As a last ditch effort he tried to put me under hypnosis, but it didn't work. The spirits had made clear only they were allowed to put me in such a state.

When I was fourteen, I moved in with my grandmother. Mom and Dad had pretty much given up on parenting me, and Grandma had a stronger personality, so they thought she would be able to crack the whip. Of course it didn't work out that way. But I loved my grandmother very much and I liked living with her. Although I didn't talk about it, she seemed to sense I had something unusual going on internally. She tried to understand me as best she could.

For my part, I felt her good soul. Also, living in her house amused me. You see her house was haunted. I was picking up on earthbound spirits a lot in those teen years, and at Grandma's I picked up Indian chants and music.

By high school I was as independent as a teenager can be. You might say I was an old soul. And I had no fear. I really mean it: almost nothing scared me. I felt amazingly confident in the spirits' guidance because they had never steered me wrong. I had begun to understand that they never would, and for this reason I never felt alone. I knew they were protecting me, and that they wanted to impart knowledge on me to be used for good. I had tuned in completely, and I was starting to open up a bit and say out loud what I saw and felt. I could be very blunt, too, because I had no filter. Not only that, I couldn't be swayed once I made up my mind. Of course this meant being labeled as stubborn or oppositional, but that didn't matter to me. I was also considered cold and distant because I wasn't interested in hugs or other physical contact. This isn't unusual, by the way. Most mediums are not the huggy-kissy type. The reason is that we can feel the person a few inches away, and by the time they get close enough to hug we feel suffocated. It's something that takes time getting used to.

As my teen years went on I began communicating with more and more earthbound spirits. When they realized

19

what I could do, they made their presence known quite often, sometimes unexpectedly. That part wasn't always welcome. Remember the movie *The Sixth Sense*? That little boy who couldn't tune out the dead, so they always were coming around and terrifying him? That can really happen if you don't know how to block them. But sometimes you don't want to block them. Instead of just annoying, a spirit might be in trouble or need to get a message across to someone in the flesh world.

In high school I sometimes received such messages, and if they were important I would pass them on. But mostly I paid attention to messages from a different level of spirits. Spirits with higher vibrations, ones that had never existed on earth. They told me information that was more profound than anything an earthbound spirit could tell me. Around age sixteen I began to feel compelled to help others with this higher information. I started volunteering at nursing homes and places where I felt people needed comforting. Meanwhile, at school I kept to myself more and more, mainly because kids didn't understand me and thought the things I said were odd. Over time, however, word got around that what I had to say could be very helpful. Kids would come to me for information they couldn't get anywhere else. That's not to say everyone embraced my abilities. When people don't understand, it can really freak them out! There are also the ones who feel threatened by what I say. I find most priests fit into this category. I know their "veil" is limited because they can't, or won't, tune in as I do. Deep down I think they know it as well, and they don't like it.

All this time I was keeping the real source of my knowledge and understanding to myself. It wasn't so much out of fear, as you might expect, but because I didn't feel any need to share it. Maybe at the time I didn't realize the spirits had become such an integral part of me, a cornerstone of my personality and the decisions I made every day. So it wasn't until I was about twenty that I told anyone about it. To my surprise, people came to me even more. People desperate to understand something, to know something. People who had sought that information before and were let down by society's limited knowledge. These were my favorite subjects: the downtrodden, the damaged, even the outcasts. I felt great compassion for them, as did the spirits.

And so I entered adulthood having matured not only in body and mind, but spirit as well. I had developed my abilities to the point where I barely thought about them anymore. Spirit contact was just a part of my life, like walking and talking. In some ways I had matured well beyond my years. Yet somehow I knew there was a lot more development ahead.

Just how much, I had no idea.

2.

Why Do I Have This Ability?

Knowing yourself is the beginning of all wisdom. – Aristotle

By the time I entered the third decade of my life, I had already asked myself a thousand times, why do I have this ability? Why me, instead of someone else? Even more important, what's it for?

At first glance, the answer to the third question seems obvious. It's for knowing things that otherwise might not be known. A psychic or medium is able to gather information without need of the physical world. By physical world, I mean all things that are picked up by the five senses we're all accustomed to using—sight, scent, taste, touch, hearing. A medium discerns not only the physical world, but also what comes from the spiritual realm—a realm just as real and present as the physical world. It may not be as observable to the living, yet it's there, make no mistake. If you need scientific evidence to convince you, just watch the news. Every day scientists learn things never thought possible even a few years ago. The Large Hadron Collider, the Hubble and Kepler telescopes, rovers on Mars and probes orbiting the moons of Saturn—in recent years all of these instruments have wowed us with mind-bending discoveries. Theoretical physicists prove all the time that what was once thought impossible is actually probable. Einstein's theories seemed bizarre a hundred years ago— until they were proven over and over again. Some of the wildest theories may be just beyond our present ability to prove, but someday scientists will build instruments to prove them as well.

Meanwhile, what better instrument for discovery is there than the human brain? The human brain's capacity to discern what isn't plainly in front of us is practically infinite. Its sensitivity to things that exist beyond the conscious state is simply amazing. This has been proven again and again. And yet most of us are content to keep the bird in its cage. We keep our mind safely focused on only the five senses, afraid to open the cage door and see where it will fly.

I suppose you can say I wasn't afforded that luxury. That *safety*. And I thank the Creator every day that I wasn't! You see I know I was given this ability to help others. I'd started to realize this as I entered my twenties, and by the time I was thirty it wasn't even a question. What I didn't know for sure was the extent to which I would use it. But the journey had to start somewhere.

For me the journey began as naturally as a beacon light draws ships safely into harbor. As I said at the end of the previous chapter, in my early twenties it started getting out that I had this ability. Up to that time I had mostly kept it to myself, which was reasonable considering I was only a child and not yet ready to handle what people might bring to me. But when I was twenty, I finally began to open up. I started by telling a few trusted friends. To my surprise, they were totally accepting of it and even began coming to me for information. As a child I never felt the need to tell people where my information came from, but as an adult I wanted people to know. I guess it was just time.

The more I opened up verbally, the more my sensitivity expanded. Having shrugged off any need to hide my ability, my antennae sort of extended and spread out. When I was 20, I moved out to California with my new husband. We had married young, at a time when I was just getting to know myself fully and starting to search for something bigger. I needed to know the bigger answers; I especially needed to understand my place in the larger scheme. My husband, on the other hand, was content with a staid life. In short, it turned out to be a bad match and the marriage lasted less than two years.

But that marriage had brought me to southern California where I began opening up those antennae I told you about. Rather than feeling sorry for myself about my broken marriage, I found myself drawn to people worse off than myself. I was especially attracted to the homeless. I've explained before that I had spent my young life looking for people to connect with on a deep spiritual level, and in California I discovered that a crucial quality was required for that connection: humility. I needed it, and the people I might connect with had to have it. And no one is more humble than the downtrodden. When you've lost everything that's when you're at your most humble. There's energy among homeless people that you seldom find elsewhere. Think about it: street people have nothing to hide. There's a kind of freedom in that. Except for the ones who are addicted to drugs or alcohol (and contrary to popular belief, a lot of them are not) there's nothing to control them anymore.

I often sat down with homeless people and listened to their fascinating stories. I learned that the homeless take care of one another. They have their own little underground system. They know what's going on in the city better than anyone else. And they know other things the rest of us don't. Their energy is different because their focus is survival. They're different spiritually. You see, these people, for whatever reason, disconnected from the political-social system, and in doing so they found their inner selves. A lot of them look to a god of some kind, yet in their own private manner. They don't need church, so the middleman is gone. They're free to develop their own spirituality.

That time in Southern California was a period of growth, a time when I was on my own and able to focus entirely on my ability and what I could do with it. But it wouldn't last. Five years into my stay there, I grew restless. I was single and living alone. For work I was waiting tables at a café. I felt stagnated, like I needed to get back on a path. The only way to do that was to move away, and I kept thinking about going back to Colorado because it seemed the most logical step.

One day I informed Spirit of this. Now, at this point I need to explain the term "Spirit." Spirit is my way of referring collectively to the group of spirits I'm in touch with regularly—my personal guiding ones, not the earthbound ones I run into sometimes. I have counted thirty of them altogether, which was verified by a Native American medicine man. Sometimes they communicate individually and sometimes as a group or subgroup. Each has its own vibration, but a lot of them work together. However they do it, their information and advice is always spot on, but not always easy to decipher. After all, spirits are not there to tell us what to do and run our lives for us. It's like that old adage told to writers and filmmakers: whenever possible show, don't tell.

In the case of my move to Colorado, I told Spirit I intended to follow through with it, unless they showed me something else. Well, Spirit did: within a month I had met my present husband, Chaas, who was in the Navy and stationed in San Diego. We fell in love and got married, and a year later we were being shipped off to Japan.

I liked Japan. There was a certain serenity about it. Even in Tokyo, a huge, bustling city, I felt safe. That was important, because I was about to have our first child. Before we left the U.S., I told Chaas we were going to have a boy and we would name him Gage. I had nothing to go on, no ultrasounds or other tests, just the word of Spirit. Of course, Spirit was right. And not only did Spirit tell me the child's sex, I was told exactly what he would look like. Chaas was still getting used to my ability, and he was astounded when Gage turned out exactly as I'd seen him. He wasn't so astounded when I did the same thing with our next child, Bryce. By then, Chaas had begun to take it in stride.

We were stationed in Japan for two years before Chaas was called back to the U.S. to serve as a recruiter in Bozeman, Montana. Bozeman was new, but at least we would be in a part of the country that felt familiar. Besides, Montana is an exceptionally beautiful place if you don't mind the winters.

At this point I had done something that might surprise you: I had more or less shut off my connection to the spirit realm. I needed to, so I could concentrate on parenting my two young boys. It was sort of like taking a vacation. Spirit didn't mind much; it understood fully that I wasn't in the mindset to continue with my progress at that moment. Now, you might wonder how I could just switch it off. People are used to psychics and mediums they see in movies and television, who are helpless to stop the information flow. It's not really like that, at least for me. I can shut it off, like turning off the power button on a radio. The radio is still plugged in, and I can press that power button again any time I'm ready, but I do have control. This way it's not disrupting my life all the time.

My "vacation" lasted a few years, while my kids were small, and then I was ready to start up again. By then I was in my thirties and had taken on a job in a construction company. I was around other people every day, and it was just a natural environment for tuning in once more. There was so much information all around me, and Spirit was glad to guide me with it once again. It was like a happy reunion.

Three years later, the whole thing took on a much more serious—and disturbing—tenor. 911 happened.

I already knew prior to that day that something big was coming. I didn't know what, only that it involved great anger and upset. That very morning I felt these two emotions very strongly. After it happened, I felt terrible confusion from the spiritual realm. Not pain or upset, but a sense of disconnect. It came from so many dying so suddenly. When the spirit of what was once a flesh-and-blood person suddenly gets violently released, it often feels this bewilderment. It can take time for the soul to realize what has just happened and start looking for where it's supposed to go. In this case, I felt an incredible amount of confusion from many, many souls.

I knew this wasn't just another tragedy like a natural disaster. This was much different. There was a shift of energy coming. Energy of defiance, of damage, of taking down. Every so often I sense angelic sadness, and this time I felt it strongly. In their way they had tried to warn us, yet we were so caught up in our daily lives that we ignored the signs. Their message hadn't been heard, and they were just very, very sad about it. It was going to take a phenomenal presence of mind to wake up from this nightmare, to heal this dark time, but first something I call demonic energy had to be overcome. A decade and a half later we're still healing.

The 911 attacks had a profound effect on me. It had a profound effect on every American, but for me it was more than just the horror and the feeling of vulnerability. For me it was a kind of awakening. Up to then I had dealt in dark energy mainly on a case-by-case basis. I knew it was out there, of course, and I knew it affected people who allowed it in. What I hadn't realized is that the darkest, most negative energy—demonic energy—can grip us *en masse*, and for lengthy periods. Whenever this cumulative energy gets the upper hand, bad things are going to happen no matter how hard you try to stop them. We humans like to refer to these periods as "dangerous times". The period leading up to World War II was such a time; demonic energy gripped most of the world then. The period following 911 has been similar. There is a general unraveling of law and order, and paranoia and hatred rule the day. Even at times when nothing significant seems to be happening the hatred is still there below the surface. And that's where the greatest danger lies.

After 911, I felt compelled to pay more attention to the negative information that came my way. It's natural not to want to dwell in that energy, but I realized I sometimes had to do just that to be most effective. I learned that humans tend to bring demonic energy upon their selves, to open the door for it to come through. Ironically, they do this by trying to ward off the very evil they bring upon themselves. Think about it. We all suffer the pains and sorrows and aggravations of everyday life. Unfortunately, we've learned to go for a quick fix, something to dull the pain, however temporary. We abuse drugs, alcohol and even our most cherished expression of love and peace: sexual intimacy. By doing so, we open the door for even more evil to enter. I'm not talking about the obvious inherent "evil" associated with self-abuse and abuse of others. I mean real hardcore evil, the kind brought on by demonic energy. Any time you let a foreign substance or even a negative mindset (violence or abusive sexual attitudes, for example) rule your body and mind, demonic energy comes to control you. This is why, for example, Tibetan monks never do anything that can potentially lead to loss of control of their body or mind. Self-control is the key to staving off demonic influences, and these monks would never give a demon an opportunity.

By the way, I'm not talking about demonic *possession*. That's a whole other level. We're talking about the simple, everyday outside influence demonic energy can have on one's life. If people could see what I've seen going on inside

31

a person who is abusing his body and mind, they'd be shocked. It's not pretty.

But getting back to my work in the negative realm, it just seemed to naturally coincide with 911 and its aftermath. I became more aware of the demonic energy that threatens each and every one of us, and I pointed it out to people who sought my help. Moreover, I began doing more than just psychic readings for individuals. I stretched out my mind, expanded the reach of my ability. I began paying attention to missing-persons cases, for example. I would open up and allow Spirit to show me things connected to these cases. I also opened up to information about fatal accidents and white-collar crime. In addition to person-to-person readings, I found myself able to do remote readings and with surprising accuracy. As long as I opened up to Spirit and let it know I trusted what I would be shown, Spirit was willing to work with me.

The result was that I got into some serious matters, and I made up my mind from the start that I would do it right or not at all. Primarily, what this meant is that I would never try to *control* the information. It probably won't come as a surprise to you that there are some fraudulent psychics out there. Not just the beach arcade crystal-ball-reading ones, either. Other psychics *do* have some power, yet not as much—or not the kind—that they claim to have. What may surprise you is that a whole lot of legitimate psychics and mediums with strong powers are mistaken for charlatans for one reason alone: they try too hard to please people. All sorts of pressures—financial, reputation, even empathy—can lead some psychics to tell people what they want to hear. They do it to be encouraging, to leave the client with the impression that all is good in their neck of the universe. This is just plain wrong. If I can't channel a client's Aunt Martha because Aunt Martha's not coming through that day, I will tell him that. It's okay to fail. The spirit realm is not something we can control. The same is true with negative information that might come through. I'm not going to mince words with my client; I'm going to tell him the truth. This doesn't mean I will hurt someone's feelings or frighten them if it's not necessary. Yet if they want the good, the bad and the ugly—and that's what most of my clients do want—then that's exactly what they're going to get.

I don't try to control what Spirit shows me, either. This is why I'm known for my accuracy and the depth of my information. I get it from a source that will never let me down, so long as I trust that source and let it show me only what it feels I need to know. I don't ask why Spirit gives me this or that information; I simply trust that there's a good reason. And as I've said before, it's never steered me wrong.

The other thing I refrain from is claiming an ability I don't have. I know exactly what I can and can't do. Every psychic or medium is different; each has one power or another, but rarely is any sensitive able to do everything, as I'll discuss in future chapters. By the time I was in my thirties I had learned what I, personally, could and couldn't do. And I had become determined to put those abilities to work in what I considered to be a crucial time. A time in which people had begun to crave a real connection to the higher realm of consciousness that exists all around us. I realized that people wanted control over their lives, as well as the spiritual balance that comes from understanding their place in the universe. I also realized they were having trouble finding their way to that balance.

Now I knew why I had been given this ability. I was meant to help people with all of these things, and I was meant to do it now. And so I entered a whole new phase in my life.

3.

Where Do I Go From Here?

A life lived for others is the only life worth living. – Albert Einstein

At some point in our lives we all do some soul searching. We seek to understand our sexual identity, our spiritual needs, even our physical limitations. We all want to know what software drives our hardware, you might say. This soul searching doesn't always occur in quiet moments of reflection. Often it happens piecemeal, whenever choices are presented to us in our daily lives. But every now and then we stop and ask ourselves the big question: is my life going where it should?

Being like you (well, that 99% anyway), I've been soul-searching all of my life. Yet it wasn't until I was well into my thirties that I finally asked myself a big question that I'd been ignoring for some time: what am I supposed to be doing with my ability? Up to then I'd just been going along living a normal life in most respects. I treated my ability as an attribute that's just there and maybe comes in handy once in a while. Kind of like a garden tool that my neighbors borrow once in a while.

But at some point I began asking myself if there was something more to this, something additional I was supposed to be doing. Actually, the question came about because Spirit had been pushing me about it all the time. When Spirit really wants me to "get" something, it can become pretty persistent. In this case, the message kept getting put in my head that I was supposed to be doing more. It became almost impossible to do anything so distracting was the badgering. And one day the answer finally hit me. I had been looking at this all wrong. I didn't just own the garden tool; I owned the knowledge of how to use it.

At this point you might be asking why Spirit didn't just come right out and tell me what to do. It's a fair question, and here's my answer: it could, but chose not to. One thing we who set out on this journey into a higher consciousness have to learn sooner or later (hopefully sooner) is that spirit guides and angels aren't there to run our lives. In fact, the opposite is very much the case. Think about it. Why would a Creator—any version you happen to believe in, it doesn't matter—put us here, in the flesh, just to act as puppets? What purpose would it serve? That's not what this existence is about. Guided only by some sensible game rules, we're mostly left on our own to enjoy the thrill of discovery and development in ways that can only be done in the flesh state. More important, we are expected to progress as beings. But more on that later.

Having said this, I will admit to having asked Spirit for a little coaching on this huge matter in my life. The answer I got back was so obvious that I should have guessed it long ago. I was simply reminded that I'm not an island. That, like everyone else, I'm part of a greater consciousness, a greater soul, if you will. That was all the answer I needed. I left my job and went into psychic-medium work fulltime.

Up to now, my ability had been deepening and increasing in breadth, and as it did I found myself stretching out even more. I'd started paying more attention to things outside my personal environment, like missing persons cases, car accidents and the like. I was shown information, only to have that same information come to light later on. It might be a color or a texture of wood or a peculiar smell. I didn't actively pursue this as "work", but simply for the sake of knowing. More to the point, Spirit was sending me this information for its own reasons, and I only spoke up about it when I knew it could help. Sometimes I warned people when I knew they were facing danger, especially people going on car trips. I always spoke up when Spirit showed me a potential danger, as it was obvious that was what I was expected to do.

I was also doing impromptu readings for people who knew about my ability. Word had gotten out, and more and more people were coming to me. It got to be a demanding side job, but I did it gladly. I loved helping people.

But it got to be too much, and I finally decided it was time to do this kind of "work" unbridled. Which meant I was about to enter a whole new world I wasn't used to, because I had never really worked around other psychics. To my credit I wasn't impulsive about it. I knew I was a novice at this, no matter how long I'd had the ability. I also suspected that, just like everything else in the flesh state, there are varying degrees of ability and intent. It's like professional athletes. Some are fast and some are strong. Then there are the ones who are both fast and strong. Some can hit a baseball travelling ninety miles an hour; others can hit a three-point basket with a defender in their face. They're all good at what they do—exceptionally good compared to the rest of us. But the types of skills they have vary, as do their skill levels.

Their intent does, too. Some professional athletes are driven by money more than others. Some crave the recognition only top-tier athletes enjoy. Others are just glad to have made it to the pros at all.

The same holds true of mediums. They're human, and humans are flawed no matter what special abilities they have. I don't mean to disparage anyone, but the fact is that some people who claim to have an ability simply do not. I think that was a bigger problem a hundred years ago, back when people really didn't understand mediumship. Back then a charlatan could put one over on her unsuspecting clients a lot easier. We all know the stories of séances with floating objects and disembodied voices concocted for entertainment, not to mention fat profits. Nowadays I think the problem is different. Yes, there are still charlatans out there. Ever watch the TV show The Mentalist, where the character Patrick Jane explains how he fooled everyone into thinking he was really psychic? There are definitely some real-life Patrick Janes out there.

Yet I think nowadays bad readings aren't so much about lying as wanting to please. People want to hear what they want to hear, and a real psychic can feel pressured to produce something even when nothing is coming through, or soft sell what the spirit world is telling her so as not to upset her client. In other words, they're not fake, just manipulative.

There's another category: the psychic who honestly has the ability, but doesn't know how to use it right. These psychics can cause confusion and chaos and misdirection. When careless, some can even be dangerous.

But there are many honest psychics out there who have strong ability and want to use that ability for good. I decided that if I was going to offer my services I was going to do it the right way, so I'd always do good and never bad. Kind of like the basic tenet of the Hippocratic oath: First, do no harm.

To do this, I decided I should observe other psychic mediums in action. I felt it was worth my time. This ability carries with it great responsibility, and I never wanted to take that for granted. So I started going to shows and meetings just to watch. And I began to notice that some of the good mediums—meaning both strong and well intended—made one fundamental mistake: they filtered what they told people. They were too eager to please, probably because they genuinely liked the people they served, but likely out of concern for their reputation, too. I made up my mind very quickly that I wouldn't do that. Whatever information I received from Spirit I would relay to my clients exactly as it came across—good, bad, ugly, and even mundane. You see I know there is always a good reason for information to come across, no matter what that information happens to be, and the client needs to hear it.

Another thing I learned was not to get too cute with what I do. I recall one medium that passed around a bag and asked people to put something personal in it. All night long it was obvious I was making her nervous, and when the bag came to me she said, "Go ahead and touch the bag." I told her I didn't need to, and went on to describe to her what she'd been doing earlier that day. She was amazed, as was the rest of the crowd, but to me it wasn't a big deal. All I did was relate what Spirit had told me. This confirmed that I didn't need any gimmicks to gain people's attention. It also reminded me that what we mediums do is not for entertainment. We're not walking, breathing Magic Eight Balls. It also reminded me that truth is far more important than satisfaction. Sometimes, I will give a client a piece of information and they will say, "No, that's not right." Instead of trying to explain myself, or back off, I'll stand by my guns. Why? Because Spirit has never once steered me wrong. *Never*. I get a lot of people who come back later and say, "You know, you were right after all." I don't gloat. I just feel good knowing I trusted Spirit and the client got the truth.

After observing at shows for a while, I felt I was ready to delve into this myself. I was now going to be what, I suppose, you could term a "professional medium." It's a term I don't like very much, only because it seems to imply that you studied a trade and therefore became proficient at it. But as far as the IRS is concerned, that's what I am. Well, okay then.

So what have I been doing these past eight years since I turned "pro"?

A lot of stuff! I attend galleries, I participate in classes, I do radio shows that are broadcast all over the world. I do private readings, either in person, over the phone or even on Skype. I have a website that keeps people abreast of what's going on. Sometimes I'm hired to do something more esoteric, such as visit a house that's experiencing paranormal activity and figure out who—or what—is haunting it. I do remote viewings and energy healing, too. Anything that requires contact with the spirit realm for assistance, I can pretty much do it.

Now, having said that last, I should clarify something. When I speak of the spirit realm I'm usually speaking of a different kind than we're all used to hearing about. Some spirits are earthbound souls that once walked the earth in the flesh. Others never existed in any physical form. They are, and always were, spirits. We'll get into this more later on, but for now I want to make clear that my ability extends to both. Yet when I talk about information being imparted to me by spirits, unless I'm channeling a specific person who has passed on but is still earthbound then I'm referring to non-earthbound spirits.

In my work I channel both types of spirits, sometimes because I'm asked and sometimes because it just happens. But here is an outline of what I do and a little about how it works:

Private readings. A private reading takes place in the presence of the client, usually in a setting they choose. Most often it's in their home, or in a place that has some meaning to them. The purpose is to help them understand something that is going on in their lives. They may be feeling or even seeing things they can't explain. We've all seen this on the paranormal reality-TV shows that are so popular these days. My methods are usually different, though. I don't use any electronic equipment and I don't really need to walk from room to room. I just sit, say prayers and wait for the energy to shift (pay close attention to this last phrase as you read on). Once it shifts, things begin to come through to me. Spirits of deceased relatives, or maybe people who once lived there. Sometimes something worse. It's nothing to be frightened of, so long as you closely follow certain procedures. But we'll get into that later, too.

Remote readings (by phone, internet, etc.). Electronic technology has opened doors for psychic mediums never thought possible. It may come as a surprise, but it's just as easy for me to do a personal reading by phone as in person. By personal reading I mean the channeling of spirits for information about the client. Clients consult me on a variety of topics, such as career moves, relationship questions, keys to their depression and anxiety. The spirit tells me what they need to hear. It never fails.

Remote viewing. If you could look inside a person's body without the help of machines and knives, you might be able to see something wrong with a certain part of that body just by color or smell. I do that. I can see what part—say, the left lower quadrant of the abdominal cavity—doesn't look right, which helps a client find answers that tests haven't been able to turn up. I smell cancer, by the way. That is one of my abilities, and not one I relish, but I do it.

Energy healing. Energy healing isn't about the body as much as the mind and spirit. In essence, you're healing the soul, which leads to positive physical effects. You might say you're helping the person heal from the soul out. My job is only to direct an angelic presence on where to focus energy for the healing. The angelic presence does the rest.

Classes. I give two-hour classes whenever I have the time. The purpose is to help others learn how to open up their own minds and develop their own innate abilities. These classes fill up fast, and I'm happy to say they work very well. I'm not the only psychic who gives classes, but I think I'm different in that my classes aren't like going to church and learning there's only one way to think, one way to do things, and no deviation. Some psychics will try to get you to do things a certain way, but I know that people often get stuck when this doesn't work. I, on the other hand, teach that communication with spirits works differently with everyone. I want the student to be raw, not molded into doing it a certain way. With certain guidelines and insight, they can figure out what works for them.

Psychic Fairs. If you've never been to a psychic fair, I urge you to try it sometime. The psychics and mediums invited to these shows do have varying abilities, but every one of them is there to confidently offer insight to the people who attend. Let's just say it's a lot harder to hide behind razzle-dazzle talk and mind tricks at a psychic fair, where there are lots of people observing, than it is at a private reading. These are sincere people for the most part, with varying degrees and types of ability. So ask questions and learn ahead of time what this particular psychic can and can't do. And above all, remember what I said earlier: a psychic can be tempted to say what you want to hear, leaving you happy and awed. Make it clear you just want truth and nothing more.

Radio Programs. I've been a guest on many radio programs over the years, from one coast to the other and also in the United Kingdom. Sometimes we're called on to give a reading, sometimes just to talk about what we do and, more important, what's coming. It's a brave new world, a changing world, one where we are rapidly learning just how powerful the mind is, and how we are connected to the universe through it. I love talking about this, and when listeners "get it," I feel like a teacher who's D-student just clicked and is now earning A's. Radio and television can be extremely helpful to all of us, but again, only if we don't use them just to entertain ourselves.

These are the things I'm involved in these days. In between, my husband and I run a small farm and raise our kids. So, as you can see, I'm busy all the time. The travel can be a pain, and the psychic-medium work can be mentally exhausting. But I wouldn't go back to my former life. I love helping people, and I love the personal contact. That's the everyday reason I love this line of "work."

The other reason—the long-term reason, if you will—is that I know I'm playing a part in something bigger. We're all evolving, sometimes faster than we can keep up with mentally and even emotionally. It's like when you were a budding adolescent and your body was quickly changing. It was a wonderful thing, but scary, too. I mean, what's scarier than having no control over your own self? But we *are* changing, like it or not, and we all need to recognize this and stop trying to go back to a simpler mindset. I believe we owe it to ourselves to develop our minds in ways that prepare us for the future, and that's partly what this book is about.

We owe it to our universe, too, for we're all just a small part of that greater whole, as I will explain in more depth later. And this is a wonderful thing. We just have to get past that adolescent angst stage, and realize that we aren't so much changing as maturing. Growing into what we were always meant to be.

And that's a good thing.

4.

Who Are We and
What's Our Place in the Universe?

It is clear that the earth does not move, and that it does not lie elsewhere than at the center. – Aristotle

Before I get into some individual lessons, I think it's important to give the reader a place mark. I'm talking about perspective. I want you to have good perspective, a clear and unhampered view of all things seen and unseen. I want this perspective to humble you, while at the same time make you understand your importance and your potential place in the universe.

I would ask you to start by acknowledging one truth: that everything is relative. Because everything is relative, we can only understand ourselves by stepping back a moment and considering everything else in the universe. It probably sounds like a lot to ponder, but it can be simplified. You see humans are atoms in a vast organism. All the stars in all the galaxies make up that organism, of course, but even the biggest things out there are no more important than each individual human. We're all part of the whole, and we all have a function.

Having considered this, you might say, "I get that. But humans are also *unique* compared to the rest of what's out there. Therefore, we have a *special* place and role. " This is true, but only to a point. The notion of our special role comes from our egos, which in turn are fed by religious dogma, which in turn stems from the longstanding belief that the Creator put life on only one planet. But what if you suddenly discovered there were other humans all over the Milky Way galaxy, or even alien races as advanced or more advanced? How would you think then? I'll tell you how you might think, and I'll bet I'm right. You'd think you weren't so special after all.

And you'd be wrong.

Why? Because you are unique and important and you play an integral part in all things seen and unseen. But remember that "relativity" word. You can think of yourself as insignificant relative to things of greater mass or power or intelligence. Yet they would not even exist without you. Everything, however large or small, plays an equal role in the universe because our universe without a single one of its atoms cannot be our universe. It's all for one and one for all. Not only that, all things are connected for eternity—or at least as long as space and time exist.

So what exactly are we connected to? I'm not sure. (Sorry to disappoint you!) No human mind can possibly conceive of everything that exists. Besides, it's not our purpose here on earth to know everything. But I can tell you that we're meant to know much more about how and what we're connected to than we already do. This especially goes for entities of the spirit realm as well as the physical realm. Yes, physical. It might surprise you to hear I'm often asked what I know about living beings elsewhere in the universe. Although I'm not a theologian or scientist or Ufologist, I'm always happy to answer based on my own knowledge and experience. But before I tell you that answer, consider the following:

Everywhere you look in the night sky there are stars with planets circling them. And we're part of every one of them. In fact, they're not just our cousins. They're us. The scientific community has known for a long time that we— you and me and everyone else on this planet—were formed from molecules that once existed only as particles floating around in space. Stardust, if you will. How that material came to be us is a fascinating study, yet it isn't completely unique.

Again I say we are unique, but not as unique as we like to think. I've pointed out elsewhere that just thirty years ago no proof existed of any planets existing outside our solar system. Since then, we've identified more than a thousand exoplanets, and we're constantly adding to the list. With billions of stars in our galaxy alone, and billions more galaxies out there, it's safe to say an incredible number of planets populate our universe. A lot of them are certain to be earthlike; we've already identified a few that appear to be in the right place for life. And that's only out of a thousand or so. Imagine how many chances there is that life exists on planets very much like our own?

It's even been theorized that the elements that formed life on Earth may have come from comets or asteroids. Living organisms, however small and primitive, may have ridden these rocky spaceships to our planet where they found the environment to their liking. In other words, *we* may be the alien invaders.

As time marches on, our understanding of the universe is accelerating. Think about it: everything we once thought we knew (e.g., the Earth is flat and everything in the sky revolves around it) was proved false only in the last five hundred years or so. That's a very short time relative to humankind's entire history. Yet before the great scientific explosion of the Renaissance, even the greatest minds insisted that Earth was the center of the universe. Today, we laugh at this notion. Imagine what we'll learn and prove to be true in the *next* five hundred years?

And that's just the hardcore science. Think about the other stuff, what scientists like to refer to as "pseudoscience." Unfortunately, this term has a derisive connotation because it's thought to refer to science that exists only in the imaginations of a small segment of our population. Skeptics point out that most UFO sightings can be explained away as natural phenomena that have been mistaken for something of extraterrestrial origin. Then there are the closer encounters, the meetings between humans and aliens, especially alien abductions. Psychologists have a field day with these cases. They believe these "encounters" are all dreamed or imagined, subconscious gobbledygook representative of real, earthly psychological issues. Yet there are piles and piles of stories out there of sightings and encounters by police officers and commercial military pilots, and even government officials as high up as presidents, who saw things that could not be explained away.

Consider this: there was a time in the not too distant past when a person risked being burned at the stake for believing things that today we take for granted. Today, we consider ourselves enlightened, science-embracing intellectuals. We don't kill people for their beliefs. We may laugh at some of them, but even then we tolerate those beliefs. And we listen and evaluate. The more we evaluate, the more it becomes clear something more is going on than just psychological flimflam.

In fact, the thought of life elsewhere in the universe is no longer a laughing matter. Probably every baby boomer recalls a time when believing in alien life was considered fantasy. Not any more. In fact, if you don't believe in life elsewhere in the universe, you're in the *minority*—at least in the U.S., Britain and Germany—according to a poll taken a couple of years ago. Think about that: 54% of Americans flat-out believe in the existence of alien life. Of the other 46%, many of those are probably on the fence.

How did this come to be? Well, for starters, everything points to it. Everything we've learned in the past hundred years about what exists beyond our planet makes it much more logical. The only thing that does not is the teachings of certain religious faiths, which is perfectly okay. Faith provides things we all need *now*. Feelings of hope, completeness, wonder and stability. The sense we are being watched over by a higher source. Yet we won't need to rely entirely on faith once a better understanding of our place in the universe is achieved. The enlightenment that is coming will answer many of our questions and fill many of our deepest voids.

So getting back to that question, "What do you know about intelligent life elsewhere in the universe?" My answer is, "A lot." I *know* life exists elsewhere. Furthermore, I know it exists in many forms, just as it does on Earth. From one-cell organisms to super-beings far more intelligent than us. It will be proved by science, too, sometime before this century is out. I'm absolutely convinced of this. We'll find signs of ancient or even present life on Mars, or maybe on one of the planetary moons. Maybe an asteroid will carry the evidence to us (we've already found amino acids—the building blocks of life—in meteorites). However it happens, it will be solidly proven by scientific methods. It might not be the life we expect, but it will be life and it will answer that age-old question once and for all: Are we alone?

That's not to say we'll find *intelligent* life right away, at least not by open scientific methods. The life we encounter scientifically—possibly one-cell organisms—will be only the tip of the iceberg. Yet make no mistake: our closer cousins are out there, too. Moreover, a select few people in the world have already witnessed this fact firsthand. My own information is that humans made contact in the middle part of the twentieth century, first by the Nazis then later by Americans. It's been kept secret for years, not because the government fears panic in the streets, but because they fear loss of power and self-determination, and are clandestinely working toward minimizing that possibility. I know this sounds like just another conspiracy theory, but I've been shown things that confirm it. So when I say we will discover other life forms what I really mean is that their existence will be confirmed concretely and openly so that all people will be privy to what only a handful of government officials and private collaborators already know.

In the meantime, most of the initial contact is being made in a way these other beings are already comfortable with: through the minds of people who have tapped into a higher vibration. That's because these "aliens" (whether they really are "aliens" at all is another topic altogether) communicate best telepathically, using energy found throughout the universe. As for me, Spirit has shown me these beings in meditation sessions. I think the reason has to do with understanding our connection to all things. Yes, life formed and evolved elsewhere, as I've been shown. Yes, some of this life is closer to us than we know. Yet we humans still think three-dimensionally for the most part, and being stuck in this gear limits our ability to explore and connect. All the while, we are in possession of a tool that's capable of reaching beyond space-time limitations and connecting with other parts of the universe. A supercomputer that was designed for this: our own brains. Through the mind, we are capable of contact not only with spirit beings, but also with alien beings made up of the same physical matter as us.

Our reality is almost like an illusion because it filters out other realms and dimensions. To lift that veil doesn't necessarily require solving physics hypotheses and mathematical equations; it's actually a spiritual thing. Remember what I've been saying about spiritualism: it's very real and it's very necessary. Scientists have already begun meshing science with spirituality, randomness with purpose. Why would they? I think it's because deep down they recognize the two are inextricably entwined.

Through my mental contact with alien beings I have been told over and over that humankind's ego gets in the way. That we must learn to set our collective ego aside in order to reach into other dimensions. Some scientists already suspect these dimensions are out there. Yet I believe these scientists, however smart, are doomed to miss the bigger picture if they don't tap into a different part of the brain.

What I've learned from other beings is that our bodies, our physical selves, don't matter much. They are vessels to carry us around in, and that's about all. What's important is the mind. The mind can tune into spirituality—which may be thought of as the interconnection of all things without need of physicality—quite easily. But this kind of enlightenment can only be achieved once we go wireless, so to speak.

When true spirituality is achieved, we will learn so much from the rest of the universe that we won't have to wait for other beings to come to *us*. We will know how to get to *them* by way of inter-dimensional travel. This is the way alien beings came to our planet, and they've been coming to us regularly for a very long time. They have been and still are camped out deep in our oceans and within our mountains. This Spirit has shown me. My own belief is that these beings are here to watch us, observe events, and see what we're up to and what it means for them and others in the universe. If things get too out of hand, they may intervene. Maybe they will see fit to teach us at some point when we're ready to accept their teachings. In the future, I believe we will understand better.

Another thing I believe is that some of these beings have blended in with us, either through swapping or altering DNA, or by cloaking. They exist all around us, but we don't recognize them unless we look hard enough. That's because they resemble us and act like us. How is this possible? Well, go back to what I said at the beginning of this chapter: we *are* them. We are part of all things, and all things are part of us. You may have heard the term "star children" or "star people." These are thought to be humans who really originated in another world, but were born here on Earth. Of course they would blend in physically, though they do have some unique characteristics like the vibrant blue or green color of their eyes. The way they *do not* blend in is with their remarkably intuitive and sensitive natures caused by being tuned into a higher vibration from birth. I believe star people exist to help push humanity toward the higher consciousness I speak of throughout this book. Based on my own experience, I even believe I may be one of them. Who knows? You might be one, too.

That doesn't mean star children are aliens. They're more like the same computer with slightly different software (maybe slightly different casing, too.) They're here because they belong here. I wish I could explain the reason, but I don't know it yet. But I do believe it has to do with the next evolutionary stage of humankind, one with the goal of looking past this planet, not just in a scientific way but a spiritual way. An awakening of consciousness. So star children were placed here to help spread an understanding of the connection between humans and the universe.

And once we understand and actually tap into this higher energy, we as individuals will become far better off. Even as a community of humans we'll be better off, for universal consciousness is our natural evolutionary path. But it begins with individual effort. It begins with each and every one of us opening our minds and becoming enlightened.

But that only happens through humbling ourselves. Yes, human beings are special, but only because we are unique—and only in a relative way. Certainly we are not nearly as important as we've come to believe. This is a good thing. It's good that we have so much in common with all the other things in the universe, including other physical beings. But this will only become apparent as we become more humble and look outside ourselves.

Keep this in mind as you read on.

5.

Human Progress: Good or Bad?

All human victories, all human progress, stand upon the inner force. – Maria Montessori

I have posited that the human race is ready as never before for a new age of spiritualism. Of connection with other realms, higher realms. I don't make this claim lightly. That kind of consciousness is a brand new frontier, one barely explored in the past. Like astronauts visiting strange new worlds, opening the mind can bring us to places we've never been before. It can—and will—teach us what we could never learn if we stayed anchored to the material realm in which we live.

The thought of this probably excites or scares you. Maybe both. If so, your reaction is normal. Anything so new and mysterious has to evoke such feelings. It's a leftover primal response handed down from our ancient ancestors. Only, strange, inexplicable things they saw in the material realm frightened them: a volcano erupting, an earthquake shaking the world all around them. Such great and powerful things must have seemed enormously important and terrifying.

In some respects modern humans are no different. We may understand the physical realm better, but not the unseen. Most people nowadays have at least a limited belief in aliens, and most of them fear that these aliens would not visit earth for good. Then there are ghosts—those are, unfortunately, the most troubling of all. Our movies and television shows are full of scary tales of vengeful ghosts and demons looking to wreak havoc on our lives.

Why are we so negative about what we don't understand or can't see? It all goes back to the primal instincts of our ancestors, who (rightly) feared the intentions of predatory animals and human strangers. We might become food or we might be victims of a takeover, so we developed this innate reaction to the unknown, a natural distrust of all things with which we were not familiar. It was all part of our survival instinct. It's the same with the cosmos. Ten thousand years ago, if you had seen a burning meteor crash to the earth you would probably think some heavenly god had hurled it at us to express its anger. And a confused earthbound spirit, unable to find its way to the next realm, wasn't merely a startling annoyance; it was purposely trying to scare us. Everything we did not understand seemed to have a negative purpose. That attitude came from our instinct to survive.

Don't let me give you the wrong impression; that same instinct serves us well today. It makes us cautious. It makes us stop to ponder what could go wrong, to evaluate the pros and cons of exploration. But it shouldn't stop us from exploring. If it did, Columbus never would have set out to prove the earth was round. Flight wouldn't have been achieved. We never would have set foot on the moon. There were so many reasons to stay away from these endeavors. The dangers seemed enormous, and in many regards they were. In 1969, for example, we not only worried about getting men safely to the moon and back, we worried about the environment they might encounter when they got there. What if they brought back some new kind of viral strain we couldn't combat? Yet we went there anyway, and by doing so we learned things about our earth and our universe we might never have learned otherwise.

As humans we have progressed to where we refuse to huddle around a fire making up stories about what we don't understand. We insist on finding out the truth through the scientific method of observation and interaction with what heretofore we knew nothing about. Thus we have sent rovers to Mars and probes to the outer planets of our solar system. We've discovered things about the giant gas planets and their moons that made our jaws drop. In doing so, we have come closer and closer to answering that question we all ask ourselves: is there life elsewhere in the cosmos? Just a few hundred years ago to ask such a question would have been considered blasphemous among the major religious movements. Today, we are more convinced than ever that the answer will be a resounding yes... and that that answer is not too far off.

So you see, we have come a very long way. Moreover, we have done so in a very short amount of time, relatively speaking. That is to say we have come a long way in the advancement of our technology and the scientific process. Science has taught us so much about what we can experience with our five senses. Perhaps predictably, this has led to a setback in religious thought. Yet the exact impact of scientific discovery on religious faith and fervor is harder to quantify because they involve two things: practice and belief. A good statistician can tell us how many people are attending formal religious services these days, but she cannot accurately tell us what's going on in the minds and hearts of these practitioners. One thing is certain: the more advanced we humans become scientifically the less we are inclined to simply follow the tenets of a religious practice blindly. For example, the beliefs of most Christian churches have changed drastically in just the past five hundred years. Christians still believe (or want to believe) in the basic tenets: a heaven and hell and one God whose son lived among us for a brief period. But examples of miracles and the devil's deeds are harder to come by these days because many of the things we once believed to be such things have been scientifically proved as mere random natural phenomena.

Is a setback in religious thought something to be alarmed about? It depends on how you look at it. We all lament the breakdown of society, as we once knew it. Even in my lifetime there has been an alarming disintegration of the extended family, with children living far away from their parents. Divorce rates are high; children raise themselves or rely on the services of outsiders to raise them. There seems to be much less civic pride and spirit, no one wants to get involved anymore. Crime rates are high, moral codes weak and ambiguous. Often these things are blamed on the lack of good religious practices. People don't go to church regularly anymore, the social scientists cry out. They don't teach their children about faith, leaving an important reservoir in their character empty. There is some truth to this, I think. Important core values—unconditional love, respect for one another, faith in the future—are all taught in most religious settings, and these values help round us out as humans.

So why aren't we going to church?

Are we going through a brief downward spiral in history, one in which we've forgotten values we will one day remember again? Was life really better back in the "old days?" when men were men and women were women and Jesus was our savior and morals and good and bad were all black and white? If so, what happened? Why don't we follow those old rules? Did the dizzying progress of the last fifty years, with moonshots and space probes and computerized everything, cause us to lose sight of what it is to be human? Did the liberal movements of the sixties and seventies throw a monkey wrench into the mix? Is this why we feel adrift?

Yes. And no.

Here's what I'm saying: We humans are travelers. We don't stand still and stagnate; we always progress. It's in our nature. You might say it's hardwired into our DNA. We can't stay still. We're restless. And it's all for the good. It may not seem that way sometimes, but what we're experiencing now is a change in consciousness. The proof is you. You picked up this book because you sensed there was something more to know, to experience. So many people are doing the same thing because they think the same way as you. It's not that religion or societal values have necessarily failed them. They had—and maybe still have—their purposes.

Yet what you can gain from what the earthly realm has to offer can never resolve the restlessness in your heart. There's nothing wrong with this. In fact, I believe that digging deep into their souls and asking what's missing in their life would best serve every person on Earth. And I believe almost every one of them would answer the same: *personal* peace. The kind that comes with self-confidence and balance. To know not only yourself as a human, but to understand your personal connection to the universe in which you live is to achieve that kind of confidence and balance. Inner peace just naturally follows.

When you last went to a formal religious meeting you probably listened to an officiant lecture about a deity. You were told what that deity wants and what it expects from you. You may have been told that the deity loves you, and that made you feel good for a while. But earthly problems seeped back in very quickly, didn't they? Soon you found yourself awash in the same doubt and confusion. Things went wrong in your life and you didn't understand why. Or maybe you didn't feel especially happy with yourself or the world around you, despite all your financial wealth and career accolades and the good grades and athletic achievements of your children and everything else you'd been taught to go after in life.

So what did you do? You fell back on your religious teachings once again. Maybe you prayed at night before you went to bed, wondering what the next day would bring, hoping your god would hear those prayers and help you. Maybe you waited to pray until the next time you got to your church or synagogue or mosque. It brought some comfort... but not enough.

Why? Because you weren't really connected. You hadn't *personally* communed with your inner self and the higher realm. What you've been doing is a little like window-shopping. You're hungry, and there are all these beautiful food items in the store, but all you've done so far is stand on the sidewalk staring in at them. The nourishment your soul needs is right in there, but you've only been given a glimpse. You need to open the door, step inside, and choose exactly the kind of food you need. But you won't get it until you open that door.

And the way to open that door is by becoming spiritual. Not in the way you may have considered yourself spiritual up to now, but on a whole different level. You must commune—I mean *truly* commune—with Spirit. There's a big difference between being religious and spiritual, and you need to understand thoroughly what that difference is. Which is what the next chapter is about.

6.

Spirituality and Religion:
What's the Difference (And Why Should I Care)?

There is no need for temples; no need for philosophy. Our own brain, our own heart is our temple – Dalai Lama

Religion. Can anything else in this world be more powerful? More moving? More controversial?

What are the two things your mother taught you not to discuss if you wanted to keep your friends? That's right: politics and religion. Mainly for the same reasons, too. Both subjects are touchy. What we believe at our core— our very heart of hearts—is so dear to us that we're willing to fight and sometimes even give up our lives to defend those beliefs. Throughout history, humans have gone to war and martyred themselves in the name of religious faith. It's that important to us.

Yet when was the last time someone was martyred for being *spiritual*? Think about that. If you're religious, you probably consider yourself spiritual, but not necessarily the other way around. Why? It's useful to start with standard definitions of the two words. Religion can be loosely defined as a formal system of beliefs and practices shared with others and usually having a spiritual base. Spirituality, on the other hand, concerns itself with human existence vis-à-vis a higher power.

Sound the same? That's because spiritualism forms the backbone of religion. Yet a spiritual person doesn't necessarily follow any one religion, or any religion at all. To be spiritual in the modern sense means you don't have to believe in a certain deity, or follow any one set of rules. You might call it a philosophy of all things seen and unseen.

I, personally, am a spiritual person. In fact I'm deeply spiritual. Yet you won't find me subscribing to any one religion. Yes, I call myself a Christian psychic, but that's because I *am* a spiritual person and I believe in the philosophical teachings of Jesus Christ. Yet, to me, every religion has its good points and its bad points; no one faith is perfectly right or necessarily wrong. Most major religions, in fact, overlap with regard to their myths and philosophies. For example, you might be surprised to learn that the Judeo-Christian story of Noah is not unique. Over history, several

70

religions have told a story about a catastrophic flood that wiped out life on Earth. Many religions also commonly believe in a god or gods that live somewhere in the sky or beyond. Organized religion offers a set of beliefs based on values to which a society can easily ascribe (e.g. if you are good you will go to heaven, and if you're bad you'll go to hell). It also offers a means of socializing these beliefs through shared experiences. Organized religions are usually full of rites and common practices through which the faith is confirmed and solidified among followers.

The trouble with religion is that it's man-made. Yeah, I know: humans didn't hand down God's word, God did. But that's a matter of faith, too. I mean God didn't hand his word down through the Bible and the Koran too, right? See where this is going? Religion—again, the traditional sense of it—requires control by humans, and any kind of human control inevitably leads to corruption. In order to have a formal religion you have to have leaders that run things and provide answers to questions the sacred writings cannot. But the deity—whichever one you believe in—hasn't sent down any spirit-emissary to do this for us, so we rely on humans. Corruption, and even innocent mistakes, inevitably follows. It's human nature. No matter how well intended, every organized religion becomes corrupt sooner or later.

There's no way to get around this if you want to belong to a formal religion. Yet this is not the case with spirituality. That's because spirituality is such a personal thing. In the modern sense of the term, spiritual experiences are limited between one person and the rest of the universe. Once you realize that your personal values and beliefs can only be determined through your own unique experiences, you are halfway to becoming a truly spiritual person. If you spend your time sitting in a pew, waiting for someone else to tell you what your values and beliefs are supposed to be (worse, what you're supposed to do about it) then you'll never truly become spiritual. At least in my opinion.

So how do you become spiritual? Start by staying away from people who tell you what spirituality is supposed to be. I know this sounds a little hypocritical, since I'm talking about it to you in these pages, but it really isn't. I'm only giving you definitions to work with. What I'm really trying to impress upon you is that, in order to be truly spiritual, you can't take your nourishment from someone else's feed trough. Once spirituality-seekers subscribe to a common set of beliefs or way of doing things, they move over into the definition of religion. Now they've collectively lost something: their own personal connection to the universe.

My only lesson to you is that you need to find your own spirituality. This is the reason I will never tell anyone what to believe. I ask every one of my students to determine for their selves what they believe. I'm not a leader; I'm a teacher, who believes in the Socratic method. I don't like to impart any more facts than is absolutely necessary for a person to "grow" their own spirituality. I like to ask questions and let each student provide their own answers. There are no wrong answers because spirituality is so very personal.

Yet spirituality is necessary for people who come to me to learn. What I teach—how to connect with the energy all around us, thereby welcoming the spirit realm and the universe as a whole into our lives—couldn't be taught to someone who refuses to accept their spiritual side. It also can be dangerous because messing with the spiritual world without the protection a higher power can lead to the introduction of demonic forces into one's life. But more on that later.

An interesting question I'm sometimes asked is, "Why do you call yourself a Christian Psychic if you don't subscribe to any particular religion? It's a very fair question, and here's my answer: my aim has never been to discount the teachings and examples of the prophets. Over history, several prophets have emerged, who claimed to be emissaries of God, or in the case of Jesus Christ, God's son. Whether or not Jesus was the Son of God or just a good man with a lot of good ideas, I say, what does it matter? It's what he taught us that counts. And he taught that love and universal acceptance of all things as our own responsibility are what we're here for. Yes, he taught us to worship one God, just as Moses and Muhammad did, but I think the central message was that we honor the higher power by respecting and loving one another. I subscribe to that way of thinking, and it has served me well in my work and in achieving balance for my own soul. So I call myself a Christian Psychic, because much of what I teach mirrors the teachings of Christ himself.

It's important to know that I don't expect people to think the same way. Far from it. So many good people populate this earth, and they come from all faiths: Hinduism, Buddhism, Islam, you name it. Almost every major religion has peace and harmony as its central goal. Peace can only be achieved through balancing the flesh with the spiritual. Because we *are* part of something greater, something spiritual that transcends this world.

So just because I refuse to call myself religious doesn't mean I'm not as spiritual as anyone else. If anything, freeing myself of any one religion has allowed me to become more spiritual because I've been able to develop and understand my psychic abilities unhindered by religious dogma and fallible human guidance. I don't care how often you pray or go to church, you will never achieve the kind of spiritual balance and real peace that's possible only without being tethered to a set of man-made rules and regulations.

Yet become spiritual you must. At least if you want to achieve the kind of balance I'm talking about. To become more spiritual, you have to tune into your *own* soul, your *own* vibration, and then apply it. It's like learning to ride a bicycle. You first have to climb on the seat and grip the handlebars, i.e. familiarize yourself with its physicality. After that, you can concentrate on understanding its energy, which manifests in balance and gravity and inertia. Finally, you learn the finer points of using the machine, and pretty soon you're jumping curbs and popping wheelies and so forth. As for learning spirituality, you have to climb into a whole different conscious state. It takes time to learn this. You're changing your brain, reprogramming it to believe *before* you see, rather than the other way around.

You can do this. I urge you to believe in yourself, because you absolutely can.

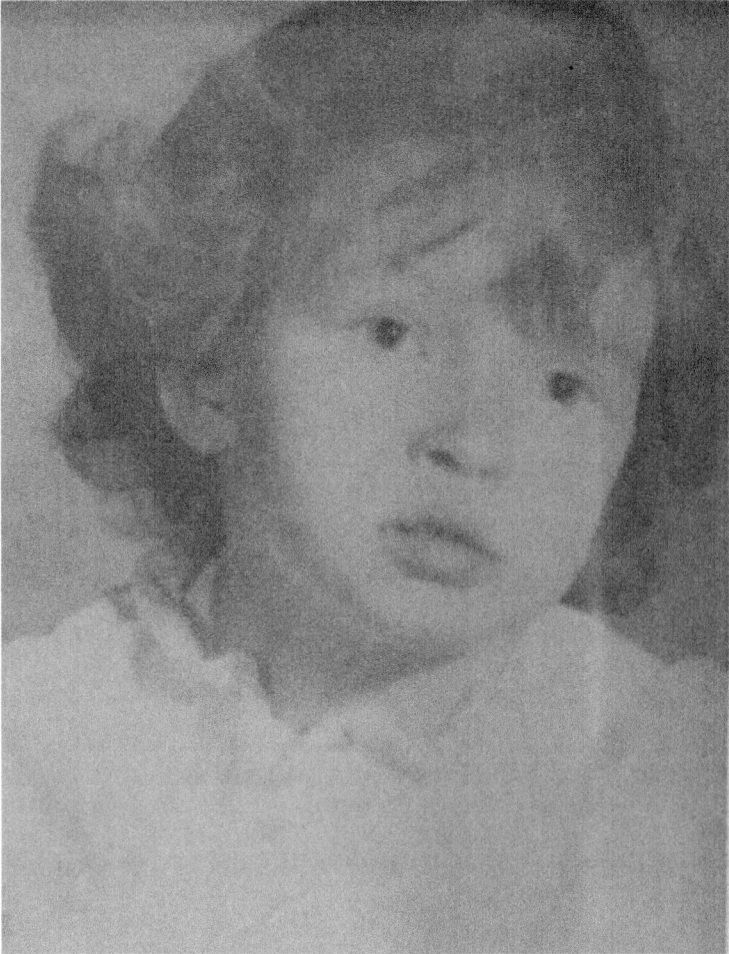

Me at age 3. I had already become aware of spirits around me. I was also causing my mother fits by wandering around the neighborhood in search of the right energy

By age 13 I knew I was different from everyone else. My parents put me in counseling, thinking my "rebelliousness" could be cured. The therapist gave up on me when I followed Spirit's advice and refused to cooperate.

As a young adult, I began doing readings for people and learning just how strong my abilities were. My elevated consciousness also led me to pay attention to things that are there in front of all of us, but which most of us ignore.

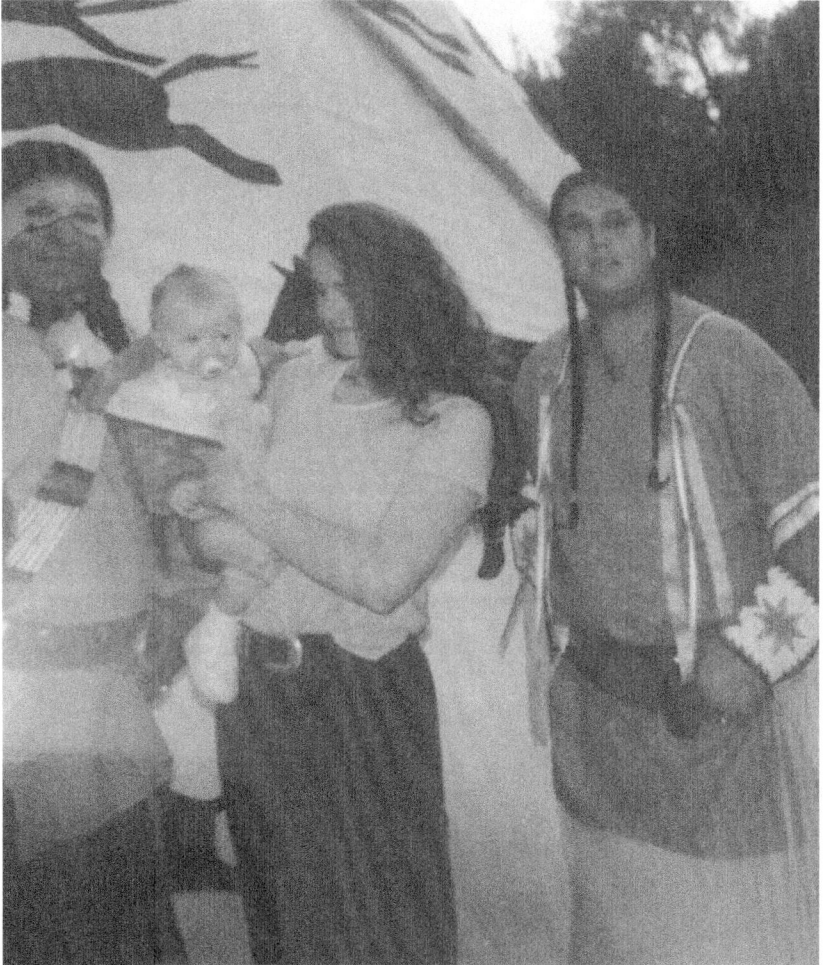

Me and my son, Gage, at a Native American event. After many years of contact with Native Americans I've come to greatly respect their way of life and thinking.

A client captured this picture on Skype a few years ago. I had just finished meditating, during which I called on Spirit. Look closely at the light and you'll see a face surrounded by a cloak. This is my main spirit guide.

7.

What Is "Balance"?

All things carry the yin while embracing the yang. – Tao Te King

A word commonly thrown around by philosophers, faith healers and even life coaches is "balance." It's obviously an important term, for it seems to be the end-goal of so many of these teachers. We all must achieve balance in our lives in order to be truly happy, they tell us. Then they tick off all the things that must be weighed, measured, prioritized and put into perspective: family, career, free time, personal reflection. All good stuff, and wise counsel, I might add.

I, too, want you to strive for balance. However, what I have in mind is a little more than the amount of time expended in daily endeavors, or how to spend your money. The balance I have in mind is much more personal. It has everything to do with your inner life. Yet it will also affect the balance of your outer life as well.

To explain, it's useful to first consider some tried and true philosophies that have been around for thousands of years. Though I'm no expert on Eastern philosophy, I have a great respect and admiration for the teachings that developed in Asia at a time when other parts of the world were still barbaric. I've said before that I find some truth and good in almost every religion; this is especially true of the philosophies of Buddhism, Hinduism, Taoism and Confucianism.

In the Tao Te Ching, it is taught that achieving balance is the way to inner peace. We all know about monks who forsake all worldly possessions in pursuit of meditation and, ultimately, spiritual enlightenment. These holy men believe that material things distract one's spiritual attention, so in order to concentrate all their energies on mental pursuits they must do away with everything not required for survival. Some people get the wrong idea, thinking they do this as a sort of exercise in self-sacrifice or punishment for sins—something along those lines. It's not really that at all. It's about living a better life by concentrating on spiritual nurture rather than earthly comforts.

Am I suggesting you do the same? Of course not! My point about the monks is that they've learned how to focus on what is most important by reducing their dependence on materiality. Think about it. We are all taught from early childhood that greater happiness comes from greater assets found in the earthly realm. Improved physical beauty, more money, more luxuries – all of these things are supposed to make our lives better. Madison Avenue has been preaching this to us since forever. It's all around us, on television, the radio, billboards. Try raising your awareness to all these sales pitches for a single day. Not just the products being pitched, but also the subliminal message underneath. The "You will be happier if you buy this product or service" message. We've become so immune to it that we don't even realize what the rat race is all about anymore. Our economy is fueled by the urge to buy things we don't really need for the sake of more happiness. And it works. Materially, we are the richest people in the richest land in all of history. We don't have to labor for twelve hours a day anymore, yet we have more buying power than ever before. We can see and talk to our relatives thousands of miles away pretty much any time we want, travel the world in hours, gratify our basic needs and urges almost instantly. What a wonderful time to be alive, right?

So why aren't we any happier? We're fat, depressed, stressed-out, anxious, lonely and spiritually bankrupt. Now, let me put the brakes on right here and explain that I'm not trying to sell you the other thing society loves to pitch: emotional therapy. Quite the opposite. I only want you to become aware of why you're seeking something more than what your present lifestyle offers (assuming that's why you bought this book). Once you start to see things for what they are—and forgive yourself for having fallen into the same trap as everyone else—I'm hoping you'll be able to fix what's broken in your life all on your own.

Start by asking yourself, what do I really need? The first things that come to mind will obviously be the ones required to stay alive. Food, clothing, shelter. But what do you honestly need beyond that? Well, humans are social animals by nature, so there's no shame in admitting we need social interaction, love and even sexual fulfillment. Many people have survived without these things for months, even years, but it's not recommended. Isolation not only makes us less content, it makes us a little less human. Remember that movie *Castaway*, where Tom Hanks gave a personality to a soccer ball? It's easy to see that happening to someone suddenly isolated from the rest of humanity.

So we need the means to survive—things such as food, water and oxygen—but we also need emotional contentment to have any meaning to our lives. What else is there? I'm talking about needs, mind you, not wants. The stuff that makes life worthwhile, good enough that we can say, "Ah, it's good to be alive!"

It's been said that life is mostly tedium and boredom, with a few nice moments mixed in and even fewer moments of sheer ecstasy. We work hard, often at a job we don't like. Yet work we must, because if we don't we will lose the ability to sustain ourselves along with the ability to retain all these material things we've accumulated and bought on credit. Yet how many of us take time—real time—to nourish our *spiritual* need? Yes, I put this in the "need" category because spiritual fulfillment isn't something we should only want. It's not a luxury it's a necessity. As humans and as animals of this earth, the Creator has given us a rare gift: the ability to experience the universe through both our spirit and our physical bodies. The trouble is we're so focused on the physical that we're barely aware of the spiritual part of us.

I'm talking about the soul, of course. We are each born with one. I am firmly convinced that all living things have a soul. Ironically, as intellectually advanced as humans are, I believe we lack the spiritual balance found in, say, a horse or a squirrel. That's because other animals lack the clutter that confuses and blinds us humans. Humans have been described as the only animal on earth that is self-aware, so it shouldn't be so hard for us to find balance, right? Yet for all our intellectual power, we still look to the material world for balance. Creature comforts, as mentioned before, are our main goal. And when those don't satisfy us we go looking for the next thing. A bigger house, a vacation home, a boat, a more expensive car. All of these things are supposed to make our lives better. But they don't, so we strive for self-esteem through outward appearances: a more powerful job, a bigger stock portfolio, a prettier spouse, fame, power—whatever other people admire and covet themselves. For this outward show of prosperity is the thing by which we all measure our lives.

And still we're not fulfilled. Why is that? Well, to put it in simple terms, outward things can't satisfy what the soul craves. And what the soul craves is universality. We've got the right idea, those of us who attend church on Sundays and sometimes pray during the rest of the week. This helps satisfy something within, but only temporarily and only to a small extent compared to what the soul really needs. So I say, make every moment of every day a spiritual one. I know. It sounds impossible. But I'm not asking you to become a monk or go live in a cave and meditate your life away.

Here's what I'm talking about:

Start by being in touch with the Creator. It doesn't matter how you define "Creator." Even if you believe the universe came into being randomly, even accidentally, you should still think about how the term "creation" fits into the equation. Most scientists agree that the stars and galaxies weren't always there. They came into being. Something— simple chemical reactions, perhaps—caused these things. That's creation, right? Whatever made us, whatever unmakes us and remakes us, is a creator in a sense. For this reason, Wiccans worship the earth and all natural things. It's not about falling to your knees and expressing words of fealty to a god you fear; it's about appreciating the highest element of creation and trying to understand your relationship with it. So be aware, and be prepared to be awed at what a "miracle" our lives are, and how fortunate we are to be able to have such a relationship with the Creator.

Acknowledge that others exist beyond the earthly realm. There is something humbling and comforting about knowing there is a spirit world beyond our own personal dimension. It's hard to experience that realm, but it's well worth pursuing. In that realm exists a host of entities that we have only begun, as humans, to understand. Angels, for example. And spirits that never existed on earth. For that matter, there are other physical beings that exist elsewhere in the universe. It's all very humbling, but comforting, too. We are never alone. We need not worry that the Creator stranded us on some tiny island among a vast wasteland of nothingness. We are among friends, even when we don't have contact with them. Respect and embrace what you don't see and you will find a kind of joy and comfort you never knew.

Let Go. Once you understand the superiority of the spiritual realm, think about what things are truly important in your life. Look around you. What have you surrounded yourself with that doesn't make your life better? Chances are you'll discover you are hanging on for dear life to things you think are contributing to your peace and contentment, when in reality they are subtracting from it. Be prepared to walk away from the clutter that gets in the way. It may be things in the garage. It may be destructive habits like smoking and drinking. It may be false friends who bring you down and make you feel worse about yourself. Maybe it's your career that doesn't fulfill your personality. Whatever it is, try to stop hanging on to these things and put a stop to the impulses that made you go after them in the first place.

You'll be surprised at how much quality trumps quantity, whether it's things or friends or personal habits.

Appreciate what you have. Now that you've resolved to get rid of the clutter that's holding you back, take some time to appreciate what's important. I know you do this already. We all do. Just do it on a different level. For Pete's sake, take advantage of the happiness these things bring! I mean, when was the last time you took the time to think about everything that makes up your life? If you did, chances are you'd discover that the most precious things have nothing to do with material wealth. Most don't even cost anything (a sunset at the beach; a view of a green valley; the sun warming your back on the porch; a star-lit night.) You have friends, relatives, a spouse, children. Be thankful you have them. Also, be thankful for the things you once had, even if they're gone forever.

Compare the small and the large. How well do you really know what surrounds you? When was the last time you sat cross-legged on the ground and watched the tiny insects go by, doing their little errands. Probably not since you were a child, right? Yet it meant something to you then, and it should mean even more now. If you look closely, you will see things you never expected. Animals, insects, even plants surprise us all the time, and they remind us that we aren't as different from them as we think. Once you've examined the small, turn to the big: the sky. We're connected to what's up there, too. Granted, we don't know as much as we'd like, at least with regard to the physical universe, but science has advanced enough to give us some idea just how fragile our place in the universe is. How deeply we are affected by what's going on out there. Understand that you are part of this huge physical realm, too. You'll find you're more like that tiny insect crawling around the ground than you ever thought. It's humbling. And it should be.

Understand your unique part in the universe. Many times I've said we are all an integral part of the universe. We all have a unique role in it. From the homeless person to the most powerful world leader, we all play an important part. You see, no matter who we are our role here on earth isn't nearly as important as we think. Yes, leaders start murderous wars and make economic decisions that affect millions. They seem awfully important, don't they? Yet in the larger scheme the power of the flesh doesn't compare to the power of the mind and soul. You are unique, and you have a role in the universe far more important than any role taken on by egocentric world leaders. As I've discussed elsewhere in this book, you are here on earth to fulfill a personal journey. To achieve goals. You have the opportunity to advance yourself, and this can be done only through your mind and soul.

Once you understand all of the above points, you will be ready to achieve balance as a person. No, you will not have achieved it quite yet, but you will have cleared the way. In order to achieve real balance you must take another journey, a journey within you and without you, to borrow a phrase. But we'll get to that soon enough.

8.

What Is Energy?

E=mc² – Albert Einstein

In this book I sometimes refer to "energy" as though it were tangible, and with good reason. Psychics not only feel energy, we sometimes see it. Sometimes we see it emanating from a person; other times we see it coming from sources of which other people aren't even aware. Working with energy—paying attention to its source and nature and drawing upon it as needed—this is a large part of what psychics do. You might say it's the way our abilities get powered.

Energy is everywhere, and in this modern age we think we understand it well. Yet I believe much of what energy is about is not yet understood. Most people tend to think of energy in the traditional sense: something released when a physical reaction takes place, such as burning organic material or consuming calories. Indeed, the sun is one great big furnace that puts out enormous energy, without which we could not survive here on earth. Yet even the sun is a finite energy source. It may seem eternal, but all stars have a life cycle, including our own star. Stars can produce only so much energy before burning out or exploding in a supernova, sending its elements skittering across the galaxy. It may take billions of years, but that's exactly what our own star will do someday.

I'm not trying to bore you with physics—believe me, I'm no physics genius. I'm only trying to make an important and distinctive point: energy already exists on its own throughout the universe. It's not just released when matter is converted via heat or chemical reaction. More important for our purposes is this fact: the energy we can tap into in this universe is as vast as the universe itself. *And*, it's not beyond our reach. Just because it's not there right in front of us doesn't mean we can't access it. We are all part of a conduit that spans the entire universe. It's kind of like the way telephone lines stretch for thousands of miles so millions of phones can access them at the same time. Or how the Internet connects millions of people instantaneously. Energy is abundant; it surrounds everything in existence.

Yet we humans tend to think in the physical sense. If it can't be touched—indeed, if it can't be seen with our eyes—it's not there. Moreover, we believe if it doesn't touch us it can't affect us. Yet in the modern age this idea is becoming somewhat problematic even for the scientific community. Take quantum theory. Recent experiments have shown that some of its strangest ideas might just be true. Have you heard that a particle can be in two places at the same time? Or that two particles can somehow communicate instantaneously light years apart, seemingly breaking the laws of relativity? What else will be proven in the next hundred or even thousand years?

One scientific theory that's been proven over and over through observation is Albert Einstein's famous equation, $E = mc^2$. This simple formula tells us that energy (E) is equivalent to matter (m) multiplied by the speed of light (c) squared. For our purposes, all we need to know is that energy and matter is the same thing in different forms. Energy can become matter and matter can become energy. What does that tell us? We see matter everywhere we look, and therefore there is energy everywhere we look. What's more, we tap into raw energy every day, mostly without even noticing we're doing it. We draw energy from sources like sunlight and moonlight and gravity, and don't even think about it. The types of energy we do think about come from readily consumable matter, such as gasoline or food. But even that matter came from energy. Sunlight, chemical reactions, molecular changes—it all came from somewhere else. Even the sun was created out of physical processes much larger than itself. It all goes back to the Big Bang.

So if we're all made up of energy, why is it so hard to believe that we humans are connected to energy sources everywhere? Other sentient beings in our universe, whether made up of matter or not, know how to tap into energy. To them it's second nature. Even earthbound spirits, which exist on the lowest plane of the spirit realm, know how to appear to the eye, or move an object without the use of physical material such as muscle or tools. They do so by tapping into an energy source. It can be as simple as fire or a battery-operated piece of machinery. You've probably heard the stories of ghost hunters whose equipment went dead when the batteries were suddenly sapped of all their power. This is caused by earthbound spirits using an available energy source for its own purposes. On the other hand, angels and pure-spirits (those that never were flesh or anything "material") don't need to tap into something, because they have their own energy source. I believe the same is true of alien beings.

Psychics are flesh and blood, and therefore we need an energy source, too. I sometimes tell students when they're just starting out that it helps to light a candle when trying to contact the spirit realm. Not that contacting spirits necessarily requires fire—it can be any source of energy—but a simple candle works well.

So why does it take all this energy for a spirit to manifest or do something we think of as physical? Think of it this way: how well are you going to do anything if you haven't eaten all day? Spirits need some kind of food, too. Just because they don't have a body to feed doesn't mean they don't need an energy source. Remember: energy and matter are interchangeable, according to Einstein. Anything that exists has to be one or the other, and is capable of *converting from* one to the other. So if a spirit is earthbound, it's going to need an earthbound energy source. That's why the temperature might drop, or a person may feel weak in the presence of a spirit. The local energy is being tapped so that the spirit can manifest locally.

The idea that energy could be harnessed in order to make something appear out of nothing has been around for at least a hundred years. Though Einstein said that energy and matter is the same thing in different forms, energy is usually detectable only during conversion from matter. We can observe things like galaxies, planets, asteroids and comets) through our telescopes, but not necessarily energy. We only see remnants of a release of energy. Thus energy is not necessarily seen with the two eyes. If we want to *see* energy, and not just its effects or remnants, this has to be done using our inner eye. Of course, energy can be felt and heard. One of the most gratifying things I do as a psychic is show students how to summon energy and work with it. For example, I recently met with a student who is a young medium just learning about her ability. It was a sunny day, and we sat outside enjoying the warmth of the sun. The sun is such an incredible energy source, and I like to take advantage of it whenever the weather allows. This particular day, I blindfolded my student and we sat facing one another. I asked her to hold out her hands. She did, and I held them lightly. As we focused our thoughts, she noticed a humming sound. Then everything went dead quiet. Next, she noted a vibration in her hands and then they sort of went numb, but not alarmingly so. She was simply sensing the energy I had summoned. As she kept her hands straight, I moved mine around them to see how she would react. Sure enough, she was able to feel the energy shift. When I moved, she moved with me, guided only by the energy (remember, she was blindfolded).

To do this you have to leave the flesh realm. It takes practice, but with the right training it's possible. You just have to get outside the physical body in order to access this kind of universal energy. But more of the "how to" in another chapter.

Energy comes from a variety of places, and some just permeates everything without necessarily having a single source. Yet it comes in only two varieties: dark and light. There's no in-between. Light energy, as you might suspect, is good energy, positive energy. It is light (as opposed to heavy), and we want it to stay with us after we access it because it feels so good and right. By contrast, dark energy is heavy and oppressive. Unfortunately, most people suffer from too much exposure to dark energy. This is because dark energy has a way of building on itself. It accumulates if it isn't somehow released. A friend of mine recently asked me to check out her office because she'd been experiencing an oppressive feeling whenever she was there. As soon as I set foot in the room, I realized a huge amount of negative energy was present. My friend deals with cancer patients, and naturally she had encountered a lot of fear and sadness and anxiety and a whole host of other negative emotions. These emotions had left behind negative energy that built up, as though the office retained it like a magnet. It took a long time to rid that room of this dark energy. We first used prayer and sage oil, then finally pushed the energy out.

As I said, negative energy tends to build up, and when it does it can wreak all sorts of havoc. It's especially hard on the soul if it builds up too much. It gets heavy and sickening. It can drive people to terrible deeds, even suicide. To avoid this buildup—and the influence of negative energy in general—you must be in balance. This is especially important when contacting the spirit realm. If you're in balance, nothing negative can come through. Demons suck up negative energy and bring it with them. But if you're in balance, they have nothing to feed on.

Tapping into universal energy is a marvelous, exciting thing the first time someone actually does it. I've seen people as giddy as a schoolgirl experiencing her first crush—only they're in love with being in concert with a greater force. This concept brings me to another important point: though I teach in the presence of my students and sometimes there is mild contact with the hands, I never transfer my own energy. There are other disciplines that believe in transferring energy from one person to the next, but this can be a bad thing—kind of like dressing a wound with dirty hands. If the one doing the transferring has negative energy, the receiver is going to get "infected." This may seem like a simplistic explanation, but there's no better way to describe it. Instead, I draw energy from elsewhere to present to the receiver. Whenever I do healing work (spiritual as opposed to physical), I attend to the chakras, which are the seven centers of spiritual power in the human body. I stimulate them, and yes, I'm using my hands to do this, though not through actual touch. But I transfer only outside energy, not my own.

Tapping into energy is a beautiful thing, and I look forward to all of my students feeling this. Manipulating energy—actually working with it—is not as easy, and it takes time to learn. Some people never get this far, but that's okay. Just by knowing how to balance their own energy, anyone can improve their life immensely. Moreover, becoming a part of universal energy is a feeling of peace and harmony that can't even be described. You have to experience it to really know what I'm talking about. I hope you will.

9.

What Exactly Are Spirits?

A ghost that will not leave when his time on earth is done has forgotten the purpose of life. – Anonymous

At the risk of overgeneralizing, there are basically two kinds of spirits: those that once existed in the flesh, which I will call human-spirits, and those that never did, which I will call pure-spirits. I'm in contact regularly with both types. Pure-spirits because I seek their guidance and human-spirits only when necessary, which I will explain further on in this chapter.

As for pure spirits, you'll be glad to know they populate the universe in great numbers. You'll also be glad to know there are certain spirits out there that are interested in you. Yes, you. Most of us are privileged to be

101

watched over by angels and pure-spirits, whose primary aim is to protect and assist us. They have been around a long, long time and their patience knows no bounds, for they've had to wait for humans to develop into what we are today. To progress to the point that we could learn to use our faculties so we could take advantage of their teachings. I believe—and this is only a belief, as I've never verified this—that our obsession with religious dogma over the past few millennia was a stepping-stone leading to where we are today. For example, in the Judeo-Christian faith we heard about human-like angels fluttering about the heavens on feathered wings and playing golden harps. They were kind and they even served as our guardians at times. They announced great moments, like the birth of Christ. What wonderful stories, right? Well, they weren't just stories. They may have been distorted and embellished (I've yet to see an angel with a golden harp), but this is what we could accept. What we could understand. In our relatively primitive—though rapidly progressing—minds, everything had to have a concrete, earthly feel to it before we could truly relate.

But angels, and the spirits that they preside over, are very real, not imagined. And being real, they are understandably not like us. How could they be? The way we look and think and act is influenced directly by living in the flesh on a rocky planet where we must breathe, and where gravity influences our bodies and movements. Angels, you might be disappointed to hear, are not beautiful in the way we imagine. But they *are* beautiful in their own way. I would like to describe them accurately, but it's difficult to do. I can only say that I observe them as light beings, but that's because they know I can accept them as they really are. For others not as well versed in the spirit realm, angels appear in different ways. There are different angels for different people. For example, one person might see his angel protector as a flying thing dressed in a white robe and sprouting wings. To other people they appear as an ordinary human being would. By the way, we've all heard the term, "guardian angel." It's true they act as protectors in certain circumstances, and for their own reasons, yet not all the time. They do other things to protect, some of which are hard to understand. But rest assured they have their reasons for everything they do—or don't do.

These beautiful entities (the term "creature" doesn't accurately describe them) are concerned with all spirits, including the souls of humans. I think they are especially concerned with humans because we've reached a delicate point in our evolution. The legions of spirits that exist as part of their "team," also do the same things, though they do not take earthly shapes as angels sometimes do. Spirits are a little more aloof, but they do love to communicate, which they do telepathically for the most part. Spirits (what I collectively call "Spirit") advise without giving away too much. They show and tell when called upon, but again, they will reveal only what they feel is necessary. How they make these determinations, I'm not sure, but I can say with certainty that their goals are always for the betterment of humans—not through leadership but through assistance, and only when necessary.

The primary role of angels and spirits is to show us the way toward better enlightenment and let us achieve it on our own. And through that enlightenment, we are better prepared for our next existence, that which we will one day reach when we have passed from this earthly life. And you should know this: they are eager to know you better. To commune with you, once you are ready.

As for human-spirits, we shouldn't be quite as eager to communicate with them. There's seldom a good reason. Contrary to popular belief, spirits of people don't happily pop in and out of our realm at will to check on us or just say howdy. You shouldn't just call on your recently deceased Aunt Martha for the sake of curiosity or comfort. It's not her responsibility to satisfy your emotional needs. Human-spirits are destined for another realm, where they typically will stay because that's where they belong. Not only do they know they belong there, they *want* to be there. It's the next step in the evolution of their soul, and a welcome place to be. It's unfair to interfere ask them to show up. On the other hand, they may *want* to deliver a message they think is important. But that's their prerogative.

Other human-spirits—well, they're not so eager to leave. There are many reasons why. Human-spirits can get confused or they might have unfinished business. Sometimes they're so attached to something or someone that they just can't let go. Remember—and this is crucial to your understanding of my message—just because a person's soul leaves its physical body and exists in spirit form doesn't mean it becomes perfectly enlightened. Far from it. Just as we fleshies sometimes get lost or distracted on a journey somewhere, a human-spirit can get confused or even afraid to move on.

I'm often called upon to investigate a haunting or even to contact a certain human-spirit that's still earthbound. Unlike what you see on television, I don't typically go into a haunted house with a team of technicians carrying all sorts of recording devices. I go in alone. I sit quietly and allow the spirit to make contact with me. And they always do because they know why I'm there. Not to play a game or harass them, but to find out why they are still here and how I can help them move on. Over the years, I've learned that these spirits can be separated into four categories: confused, motivated, angry and fearful.

The first category, confused spirits, are the ones who just can't find their way. Something happened at the time of death that threw them off the path to the realm where they were destined. I don't personally believe heaven and hell are places; I believe they are states of consciousness, and each and every soul has the capacity to arrive there if they are ready. In other words, you don't just show up at some pearly gates, or fall into a pit of fire and brimstone. You move yourself to another level of consciousness – the one you have prepared yourself for while here on Earth. An earthbound spirit, on the other hand, may be unable to take even the first step toward that realm.

Why? Maybe the person was killed suddenly, or committed suicide and thinks she's still alive. Maybe she simply hadn't accepted the idea of an afterlife, and therefore stubbornly clings to this world. Whatever causes the confusion she thinks she's still alive. She hangs around places or things with which she was familiar in life, or visits people who meant something to her. Eventually, she may come to realize she's no longer among the living, but by then the path will be out of sight. Now she is lost between two worlds—a sad state indeed!

The second category of earthbound spirits I call motivated because in life these tended to be the strong-willed, take-charge types. When they die, they still have that makeup in their personality (oh, yes, ghosts do have personalities!) and so they continue needing to get involved. A strong-willed grandmother, for example, may feel the need to hang around and watch after her grandchildren or comfort her family. Motivated human-spirits may have loved so strongly in life, and had such a need to nurture and protect, that they just can't bear to go away. So they hang around, waiting for an opportunity to help where they think they can, such as when someone is sick or needs to figure out a personal dilemma. They thrive on this, which is a wonderful thing in a way. Yet it's really not good for them— and often not good for the living, either—and they need to move on because they have their own soul to look after.

The third kind is the angry human-spirits. Unfortunately, these are the ones that populate most of our fiction: the vengeful spirit hell-bent on wreaking havoc on the lives of the living. It makes for an exciting plot, but this stereotype gives ghosts a bad name, and it's the main reason so many people fear ghosts. For the most part, even angry spirits can be dealt with in a reasonable manner. I find that a lot of them have hung around because something is eating at their soul. Maybe they want to expose their murderer, or they want to harass people who made them miserable in life. Other angry spirits were extremely materialistic in life. They loved their money and their things more than they should have. So a man who built his dream home dies, but refuses to give up that home. Soon after, a living person moves in. Who wouldn't be upset?

As I said, even these angry and vengeful human-spirits can be dealt with. I do it all the time. Believe it or not, I've sometimes offered to take a haunted item out of someone's home or place of business, knowing that it's the only way to relieve my client of the ghost that's bothering them. I've hung paintings on my porch that I knew were haunted. I don't recommend you do this yourself, but for me it works. Once I make clear to the ghost attached to it that I won't bother him so long as he doesn't bother me, we co-exist just fine.

Lastly, there are the fearful human-spirits. Usually, these are ghosts of people who did dark things in life, and who worry about retribution in the afterlife. They may fear the Hell that was described to them in church, or some other dark punishment. Whatever it is they fear, they refuse to move on. They refuse even to look where they might be going. They believe it's safer to just stay put.

Whatever the reason for staying, earthbound ghosts just don't belong here. Whenever I'm called upon to investigate a haunting, I always encourage any ghost I encounter to move on. Often, I can convince even strong-willed human-spirits to leave, but not always. Some human-spirits can only be pushed out of the place they're haunting, but they still hang around this realm in some form and with the same stubborn attitude as before. Some hang around a long time, even centuries. There are reports of medieval monks and even Roman centurions haunting ancient places.

Yet most souls do move on after their physical body dies. Most, in fact, are eager to start that new existence. The reasons have everything to do with preparedness. They accept—either at the moment of death, or right before it—that there's another place they should embrace. Just what realm they will arrive at depends on the preparation they did while living. I don't mean going to church, necessarily. One can prepare just as well by becoming truly spiritual, seeking better understanding of one's self and one's place in the universe and putting that knowledge to use while in the flesh. Respecting the earth, helping other living creatures, finding what is important and embracing it—these are all ways to prepare. When our time comes to move on, we'll be ready and the journey will be smooth.

In the meantime, it's wise to remember that earthbound ghosts were once people. They had their flaws, but most were actually good people in the flesh. And they all had one thing in common: they wanted to be respected just like everyone else. So think of them much like you do the living. Don't bother them unnecessarily. Certainly don't provoke them. They're not toys. They're not meant to be the subject of games or curiosity. Most would just as soon be left alone. And if you truly care about the dead, the last thing you want to do is try to keep them hanging around.

On the other hand, sometimes there will be a good reason to contact the dead. In that case, just understand that they don't always want to come around. If you seek help from a medium, and that medium says the particular spirit you are trying to contact isn't responding, leave it alone. And know that this is probably the best news you could have heard. For that spirit is embracing its new existence in another realm, one where he or she belongs.

10.

Are You Psychic?

Not only does the psyche exist, it is existence itself. It is an almost absurd prejudice to suppose that Existence can only be physical... – Carl Jung

Part of what I do is helping to develop psychic abilities, so naturally I get a lot of inquiries from people who believe they may already have psychic tendencies. Typically, I will get a message like, "I 've been experiencing things since childhood, but never wanted to believe it. I can't ignore it anymore. Can you help?" Sometimes they only want to understand the phenomenon because they're scared or don't know how to control it. Others have already embraced their ability and seek my guidance. These people I work closely with over time, so I get to see a lot of incredible things.

You may suspect you're psychic as well. You may even suspect you have mediumistic abilities—the ability to contact the dead. Maybe this is why you're reading this book. If so, I applaud you for taking the next step in your development. Even if you're merely curious, or just want to understand the phenomenon in the context of all things connected to higher realms, I still encourage you to make every effort. But before you go any further, you need to understand what this ability is all about.

The term "psychic" derives from the word "psyche", which refers to the human soul or spirit. Other definitions of psyche refer generally to the human mind. A psychic is someone who is able to receive information telepathically or clairvoyantly. Thus, a true psychic gathers sensory information using a tool beyond the five senses—his mind and/or soul, depending on one's definition. For our purposes, we'll define "psychic" simply as one who "sees with the mind."

Most of us are born with some level of what I will term "psychic awareness." Psychic awareness is an innate sensory tool hardwired into every human brain. It's the thing that makes us suddenly aware of someone in the room when we haven't even turned around to look. We just "sense" that they're there, even though we haven't seen or heard them. Something like this comes mainly from thousands of years of evolution, whereby our subconscious minds have been trained to "know" things that help protect us. Psychic ability, on the other hand, is the ability to know what we have no way of knowing in a purely "natural" way. Predicting a future event unconnected to our everyday experiences, for example, or "seeing" something completely outside our physical environment.

Mediumistic talent—the ability to communicate with ghosts—is another thing altogether. It requires a whole other set of skills that aren't very common. You're either a medium or you're not. Yet it's not uncommon that a person close to us dies, and we have some sort of communication afterwards. Grandma shows up beside our bed the night after she dies to say goodbye, for example. That doesn't mean you're a medium. It only means you're sensitive to— and accepting of—the spirit world enough to make a spot communication. A medium can do it at will, and with strangers. Not just once or twice in a lifetime.

Most people who come to me don't know what a real psychic or medium is, yet they're convinced they have this ability. Even if I take what they tell me at face value, I don't automatically assume they're psychic. Far from it. Believe it or not, when it comes to this sort of thing I'm the world's biggest skeptic. You see I've been a psychic since before birth. I've spent a lifetime living with this ability, and I've gone to a lot of effort to learn and progress so that I could make the most of it. When someone comes to me claiming to be psychic, my attitude is, "Okay, show me." Not just once, either. I want to see what they can do over time. Because this person might not be what they claim, no matter what they tell me up front.

Why? Well, obviously they might be embellishing or outright lying. Unfortunately, too many people are eager to get into the "game" of taking people's money in exchange for telling them what they want to hear. I also meet a lot of earnest people with little or no ability that have convinced their selves that they do have ability. They might just have an elevated level of psychic awareness, or they think they sense things that they really don't. For example, they may see shadows out of the corner of their eye, but that's all they are, shadows.

One of the first things I may ask is, "Have you ever been tested?" What I mean is tested by a person or group experienced in things of this nature, not just a friend or relative. Usually, they haven't—otherwise, they probably would not have come to me—but sometimes they have and they've heard that I can help them develop. But for the majority of cases, I find that the client has no idea what their ability is all about, or how deep it goes. Typically, they have experienced one of the following:

Déjà vu: We all know what déjà vu is: that feeling that something you're experiencing now has happened before (in French the phrase means "already seen"). Not much is known about the phenomenon. Scientists try to explain it away as some kind of glitch in our brain's processing gear, but it's so common, and the feeling can be so strong and everything else with our health can be so normal, that this hardly seems a good explanation. Theories among a number of paranormal researchers attribute it to reliving a past life experience or precognition. My own interpretation is that déjà vu may derive from tapping very briefly into another dimension, where one experienced this same set of circumstances already—only in another "time zone."

Whatever causes déjà vu it can be an indicator of sensitivity beyond the usual human kind. Most people experience déjà vu in their lifetime, but some experience it regularly. If you're one of those, you may have a budding ability. Take notes, keep track of the whens and wheres, and pay special attention to the circumstances that cause the feeling.

Dreams: Dreams are an even more common indicator of potential psychic ability for most people. We all dream, and regularly. Most of our dreams we don't even remember, but for some people dreams are so vivid that they wake up recalling even the minutest of detail.

At psychic fairs, I commonly meet people who've been having dreams about meeting strangers. The strangers tell them things that mean something later on. Or the person might dream of a dead relative or friend with a message. Some even tell me about going places in their dreams, places they don't recognize, or places they do recognize, but which are very far away. I pay particularly close attention to these dreams because they can indicate astral projection. Astral projection is a phenomenon where the soul leaves the body temporarily to travel to another place.

In many cases, the client was visited by a dead relative or friend who showed them things. These things are supposed to have some meaning, though the client hasn't yet caught on to that meaning. For example, a spirit might come to them in a dream, showing a color or a number—something that means little at the time, but turns out to be significant later. It's not unusual for someone to dream of their own death in an accident, which causes them to avoid taking a plane flight that crashes, for example. Where this message came from they can't say for sure, but it was strong enough to make them act.

My advice to the ones who continue to get messages is to write everything down then wait. If the energy and the patterns of information stay consistent then it's safe to say something is coming. Sooner or later the message usually does comes through, often when they least expect it. They come back to me with their story, astonished at how the whole thing played out. But when they think back, the message—and the way it was conveyed—made perfect sense.

Which raises an important side note: information gathered in psychic ways can seem convoluted and just downright murky at first. It can seem like a game, a puzzle being handed to you one piece at a time. I don't know why this is, but I've often felt it's because we exist in the flesh to progress through the exercise of free will. After all, if a teacher gave her students all the answers then the student would never learn. Of course, it's possible spirits just communicate naturally this way.

It can be frustrating (even for me!), but I assure you, answers do come through. Train yourself to write down your dreams as soon as you wake up in the morning. Look for patterns. If you think you're unusually receptive to information coming from beyond the veil, take the information to a reputable psychic or medium that can help you decide if you really do have unusual sensitivity.

Seeing ghosts. I've said before that seeing a ghost doesn't necessarily mean you're a medium. You don't need the powerful sensitivity of a medium to see a ghost. You only need the right circumstances and an open mind and they may come to you. Most of us, in fact, know someone who has seen a ghost. The most common sighting is of a residual haunting, which is like a replay of something that occurred in life. Thus you may see a woman dressed in nineteenth century clothes gliding along a hallway and disappearing through a door. It may happen to you once, or many times. It may happen to many people. But it's always the same action, and she never seems to notice your presence. That's because this ghost is simply replaying something she did in real life over and over.

In other "hauntings" the ghost does interact with the living in some way. Eye contact or some form of physical contact is made. The ghost may even speak. This doesn't necessarily mean the living person with which the ghost communicated is a medium. It only means that that particular spirit, under those particular circumstances, was able—and willing—to come through to that person.

A true medium, on the other hand, is able to receive messages regularly. And spirits know this. Somehow, they are able to pick a medium out of the crowd and zero in. They realize this person has the "gift" and they are eager to pass on a message. Similarly, the medium is able to call forth spirits with a relative ease with which most people cannot.

You might say that when it comes to communicating with ghosts the average person has a phone system equivalent to paper cups and string, whereas a medium has a satellite phone.

If you are in regular contact with spirits, and have been for some time, you may be a medium. Keep track of all the circumstances in which you were in contact with the dead and bring this information to someone who can verify your ability, assuming verification is what you're looking for. Just as important, you may have this unique ability, but haven't yet learned how to manage it. Ghosts can drive you crazy if they're always popping in and out when you don't really want them to. And they will, believe me, because they're just as thrilled to find someone who can hear them out! It's just as important that you learn to shut them out at times so you can get on with a normal life. So you see, you might be a medium, but there's still a lot more to learn.

Other psychic phenomena: You may find yourself unexpectedly picking up information around people. It may make you uncomfortable, even physically ill, to be around a certain person, but you have no idea why. You may even get sensations when in a particular place. For example, you might be hiking a trail and suddenly sense great anguish followed by pain, only to learn later that a bloody battle took place at that exact spot centuries ago, or another hiker fell to his death there.

On the flip side, you may be sitting in a restaurant and suddenly have an overwhelming sense of danger. You hastily pay the bill and get out of there fast. Later on that night, you hear on the news that a car drove through the front of the restaurant, hitting several people in the exact area where you'd been dining ten minutes earlier.

This isn't coincidence. People do sense the future. I've done it myself many times. I also sometimes see things that others cannot. I'm often called upon to do remote viewing, which is calling upon Spirit to show me where something is misplaced or where a missing person might be. Recently, I helped locate a body in a murder case. Spirit showed me several scenes in a remote area I'd never visited before—an area miles from where the police had focused their search. Volunteers, acting on my descriptions of the terrain and streets and buildings, were able to find the place. A short time later they discovered the body.

If you sense things or events—past, present or future—you may be psychic. Again, I would recommend that you get tested by someone who knows how. Then start learning how to make the most of your ability for the good of humanity.

Which brings me to my last point. If you are a psychic or a medium or both, you have a gift. I know the term "gift" has been thrown around so much that it's almost become cliché, but it truly is a gift. It may not seem so at times— believe me, it can feel like a curse on a bad day! But being a sensitive means that doors to other worlds have been flung open for you. Your life may be enriched in ways others can only dream. And what better way to enrich your life than to use that gift for helping others? Of course, the flipside is also true: If you choose to use your gift strictly to enrich your pocketbook and your ego, you are in for a difficult life. I hope you choose the right path.

And if it turns out you aren't really a psychic or medium don't be disappointed. The fact that you've experienced things is evidence of an open mind and heart. You are already well on your way to achieving higher consciousness, which should be your main goal in the first place. And what the rest of this book is all about.

11.

Becoming Aware

The key to growth is the introduction of higher dimensions of consciousness into our awareness. – Lao Tzu

In the previous chapter, I posed the question, "Are you psychic?" If you've been tested and it's been determined that in fact you are, then you will probably have a keener sense of what follows in this chapter. Yet you should read on, because being psychic doesn't necessarily mean you've reached your potential, and becoming more aware is vital to your progress. As for the rest of you who have no known ability, this chapter will come in handy. In fact, I don't see how you can go any further without reading and absorbing its message.

If you're like me, you wake up every morning looking forward to a good cup of coffee and the morning headlines. You want to know what's going on in the world, in your state, in your town. You may sit at the breakfast table with your family and compare notes on what's ahead for the day. You look out the window at the weather, at the condition of the lawn, and so on. All day long you gather information, often unconsciously. Being aware is what we humans are hardwired to do.

In fact, it's what all animals do. For our non-human friends, being aware not only impacts quality of life but survival itself. After all, an animal in the wild that isn't aware of its surroundings may soon become dinner for a larger animal.

I think we all agree that being aware is a good thing. It keeps us from getting into a traffic accident when the light turns red, or burning down the house by forgetting to turn off the stove. It's good for less dramatic things, too, like keeping up on trending styles of clothing.

But how aware are we, really?

Remember that Disney movie about Pocahontas, where she sings about rivers and trees and animals being her brothers? Most people, I think, took those lyrics to be symbolic—simply a way of saying, "respect the earth." That was part of it, but it goes much deeper. I know this because

I've been close to Native Americans and I understand where they're coming from. Native Americans who have held on to their culture usually have a much deeper relationship with the earth—its flora and fauna, even minerals—than the rest of us. They understand that everything, organic or not, has a life force. More important, they understand and *feel* the connection between that life force and their own.

Because they are aware.

Truly aware. In ways most others are not. Even the crunchy types, who hike the trails of the world seeking communion with nature, seldom come close to this level of awareness. Being aware is something you must practice everyday, until it becomes second nature. And it doesn't involve just knowing the headlines or memorizing the names of trailside flowers and plants. Being aware means getting to the very basics of all things seen and unseen, knowing them intimately by sensing common patterns and the forces from which they're derived.

And most Native Americans are—or were—astonishingly good at this. That's because they always lived so close to nature, close to Mother Earth and all her cosmic cousins. Unlike other civilizations, they didn't try to escape the natural world by hiding in villages and cities. They embraced the earth every minute of every day. They loved and respected all things, even those they had to kill for food.

It all came from awareness. Awareness of their surroundings and their place in those surroundings. They took time to fill their senses in ways the rest of us never do. It became a daily practice as common to them as eating and sleeping. Sadly, a lot of non-Natives laugh off this way of life as silly and pretentious. Yet how many times have we been awestruck at the movie-Indian who senses a change in the weather simply by observing what the animals are doing, or tracks a man by seeing the minutest changes in the environment? This all comes from awareness.

What I'm asking you to do is even deeper than that. And you can do it.

Native Americans and other cultures that value communion with the earth and sky also value things untouched and unseen. An example is the vision quest of Native American cultures, a rite of passage for boys to become men. In some Asian cultures meditation became a daily habit for those seeking enlightenment. Interestingly, in modern Western culture meditation has become more mainstream as our society reaches the breaking point with all its stress and fear. Meditation can relax the body and mind. It's also the doorway to higher consciousness, though most meditation sessions aren't really designed for that. But this we'll save for later.

For now, I want you to understand that awareness is the first step toward enlightenment and a connection with higher consciousness. Have you ever wondered what it must be like to die and go to a place like heaven where peace and harmony and love are with you every minute of every day? I trust you have, if the religion you follow teaches that heaven is your reward in the afterlife. Without going into the pros and cons of this blanket belief—for it's much more complex than what you've been taught—I want you to know that such peace and harmony and love can and should start here on earth while you still exist in the flesh. It begins with awareness, which is not only the first step toward higher consciousness, but has a great intrinsic value as well. For the rewards are phenomenal.

Here, I could go on all day with examples of what to be aware of. Sit on the ground and watch the grass grow, or observe the teamwork of ants collecting food. Watch a squirrel in the early fall gathering nuts and seeds for winter. Look out your office window: what is the sun's position at 9 a.m. this morning and what was it at 9 a.m. a month ago? Listen to your favorite song, but this time pay attention to the bass line rather than the whole mix of instruments. How did that bass line form the backbone of the music? And how did the rest of the instruments complement it? Experience things you can sense with your five senses. They can be the most mundane things, and probably should be. Because it's the things we consider ordinary and mundane that we tend to take for granted, and thus ignore. Yet they are just as important—and in some ways more important—than that to which we normally pay attention.

Some of these awareness exercises might sound silly, but they really aren't. Albert Einstein, one of the greatest scientists of all time, revolutionized our thinking about the whole universe by first observing the environment around him and wondering. Only then did he apply complex mathematics for verification. But it all started with just being aware.

What Einstein found—and what we all can and should discover—is that everything is connected; everything works together as a whole. We're all cogs in the machinations of the universe. Which makes us much more alike than unalike, and by "us" I mean things unseen as well as seen. Einstein's famous thought experiments, which led to his theories of relativity that blew away everything that came before—even Newton's theories—started from awareness. Granted, he had incredible powers of concentration. He could do these thought experiments for hours at a time. Thus he could get in an elevator and wonder what it would feel like if that elevator were lifting him through space where there was no gravity, which in turn led to the question of why acceleration felt the same as gravity. Or he could imagine himself running beside a beam of light that keeps moving away from him no matter how fast he goes, and wonder why. I'm not asking you to spend hours and hours on thought experiments (who has the time, right?), but practicing better awareness every day will bring you to a presence of mind that will enable you to take the next step toward higher consciousness.

Take time to look around you. Listen. Smell the air. Know what surrounds you, but try not to just accept what is. Instead, ask *why* it is. And *how*. You might be surprised at the answers that come to you. When you feel comfortable that you're more aware of your immediate environment, take the next step. Think about the earth and the planets. Then move onto things unseen. It doesn't matter what you come up with. It might be the nature and composition of alien beings, or the smell of outer space. The point is you must train your mind to take in more than what you have in the past.

These exercises will enrich your life immediately. Moreover, they will help prepare you for reaching beyond the physical realm, which is the natural evolution of awareness, as you will see.

12.

Choosing A Psychic Assistant

I am indebted to my father for living, but to my teacher for living well. – Alexander the Great

By now you've figured out that this is a book about learning. Its aim is to (hopefully) enlighten you about who you are, what we all are, and where we're going. Most of all, it's meant to raise your consciousness above the materiality of this earth, for there's so much more to tap into now and in the next realm.

A more specific aim of this book is to teach you how to do this on your own. Yet I recognize that getting started in an endeavor this unfamiliar requires some assistance from a good instructor. I'm talking about psychic mediums. A good psychic medium can help open up the universe to you by demonstration, guidance and encouragement. Whether you simply want to contact someone important to you who has passed on, or you feel you have some mental ability yourself, a good psychic medium is essential. The trick is finding the right one.

But let's first talk about what a psychic medium is. Actually, the phrase "psychic medium" can be misleading. A psychic and a medium are actually two different things. A psychic is a seer, a person who can see faraway events or things. They are also known as clairvoyants, since they often see the future. A medium is a person with the ability to contact the dead. Not a ghost hunter with recorders and cameras and other gadgets, but a person who can communicate with earthbound spirits using only the mind and senses. Still, the terms "psychic" and "medium" are often used interchangeably. What you need to know is that they are two different abilities, and it's rare to find someone who has both.

Having explained the difference between the two, you will know which kind of guide you seek. That's the easy part. The hard part is knowing which are good and which are—well, not so good. The sad truth is that a lot of people out there claiming to have "the gift" really have little or no ability at all. In fact, I would estimate that ninety percent of psychics and mediums either exaggerate what they can do or flat out lie about it. There are lots of reasons for this, too. Some have a certain amount of sensitivity, but not as much as they think. This error can be caused by a lot of different things. For example, some people are amazingly good at deductive reasoning (think Sherlock Holmes) and they assume they can "predict" events. Others just have a keen intuitive sense. They pick up on things about people from their body language or voice inflections and even handwriting styles. These people might convince themselves that there is something paranormal about what they do, when in reality they have no sensitivity to anything beyond the earth realm.

Then there are those who are flat-out charlatans. These types are well aware of their deductive and intuitive abilities, and have parlayed them into a profitable circus sideshow. They're entertainers, no more real than the man who guesses your weight, or Madame Something-or-Other with her silly crystal ball. Yet they're masters at putting on a show based on information learned ahead of time, or gleaned from the audience or person by gently pumping them.

Even among real psychics and mediums you will find a wide variation in ability and kinds of ability. I've met a few who were astonishing in their ability. These sensitives quietly go about helping others without much fanfare. They don't seek attention; in fact, most shy away from it. Yet when called upon to put their ability to work, they do so for the good of those they serve and humankind in general, not themselves.

So how do you find a good psychic or medium? Start by using your own powers of deductive reasoning, intuition, and most of all, common sense. Start by asking yourself, "If I were one of these people, what would I do? If you answer, "Turn it into a television show, make loads of money and live in a Beverly Hills mansion," you probably shouldn't be wasting time on this book. If you say, "Help people by giving them hope of an afterlife," then you're running the danger every person seeking a sensitive's help runs. Like any good mentalist, a phony sensitive knows there are two questions all humans want answered: are we alone in the universe, and is there an afterlife? As for the second question (the first is dealt with elsewhere in this book), a talented mentalist preys on a person's need to hear a definite "Yes." Most people who come to psychic fairs or participate in television psychic shows are looking for concrete evidence to support the existence of an afterlife. They've already read or heard that it exists, but they need to see supportive proof. What a wonderful set of circumstances for a fake medium! You'd think the people at such shows would be wise enough to avoid this trap, but as every mentalist knows, when the emotional side gets switched on people will believe anything. You see they crave confirmation so badly that they don't pay attention to the warning signs.

I'm here to tell you those warning signs—and to tell you to keep your antenna up. Why? Because what I do isn't a circus sideshow. It's not designed for entertainment. After living with this ability for nearly half a century, I've come to understand that no real psychic or medium would choose this profession. You don't wake up one morning and say, "This is how I'm going to make my living." It's not an easy life, and for those who do it with honesty and the right intent it's not all that profitable, either. In fact, the only sound reason for charging people for our services is so we can help as many as possible without going hungry.

The best way to find out if a sensitive is what he or she claims to be is to avoid blanket referrals. If a friend tells you, "I heard so-and-so was good," ask them why. Something so complicated as clairvoyance and channeling can't be summed up as good or bad, like a good plumber or carpenter. Your friend may have read it on a website, or seen ads that claimed this particular psychic was good. She might have even gone to that psychic, and having believed the hype, interpreted what the psychic said as accurate when it really wasn't very accurate at all. You might ask your friend what the psychic did, what he said and how he arrived at what he said. How did he operate? Did he ask a lot of questions? That's a surefire way of telling a good psychic from a charlatan. Too many questions usually equate to pumping for clues—something a phony does well.

I'll use myself as an example. When I host a gallery, I don't stand in front of the audience and start channeling little messages:

> "I'm getting a nurturing sign—someone's mother is coming through. I'm getting the letter 'C.' Does anyone have a mother or grandmother who has passed on and whose name started with the letter 'C'?"

No, I don't work that way and never will. Why? Because that's not the way Spirit works. I'll generally ask one person to give me a name. One name only, a first name. This is a person I have never met before, who has never registered or written down any information about herself, who hasn't spoken to any handlers who then pass information on to me. All I need is a single name, so I can ask Spirit for information about that particular person. Spirit always knows whom my client is referring to, even without a last name. I don't ask any other questions, unless something gets confused. Spirit doesn't need any other information.

Once I have a name, I communicate with Spirit mostly in things of the senses—images, usually, but often smells, sounds and even tastes. When appropriate, Spirit will give me a feeling. It might be an emotion, or it might be a physical sensation, such as a pain in a certain place. Through all of this telepathically gathered information, I can tell my client what Spirit wants me to tell him or her. I don't control what comes through—Spirit does.

By the way, you'll never see me turn my back to the audience or close my eyes. It's not necessary. I can channel information just as easily with my eyes open. This connection to the spirit realm has become so second nature to me that I know whatever comes through will not only be truth, but all the facts Spirit—for whatever reason—deems appropriate to reveal. And my readings are always very accurate. If they don't seem accurate at the time, that's okay. Nine times out of ten I will hear back later—after my client has verified through further investigation that in fact I was right and they were wrong. The other thing is that I'll only tell my client what comes through—good, bad or ugly. I don't whitewash, I don't try to explain or interpret and I certainly don't try to wow them with my skills. I can't stress this enough: *a good psychic or medium is not there to entertain people or make them feel good by giving them false hope.* What I do—what anyone claiming to be a sensitive does—is serious business. There is so much at stake: emotions, belief systems. It's not to be taken lightly. That goes for the client, too. If you want to know something, but can't live with the answer, it's best to avoid asking. You'll only get the truth from someone like me.

Which brings me to another point: there are some sensitives out there—a lot of them, in fact—who are genuine, but they're so afraid to offend the client that they soft-peddle or whitewash or even stay quiet about information that comes through. This is information manipulation, and you don't want this kind of psychic or medium either. What good is plunking down your hard-earned money for lies and misguidance? Would you want your doctor to tell you that lump is just a harmless cyst when he knows it's really cancer?

Yet sensitives are human, and they either get too emotionally involved with their clients or else they're afraid they'll lose business if they aren't making everyone walk away happy. Not a good thing for you.

And not a good thing for the progress of higher consciousness in general. Like any other phenomenon, the hoaxers and self-absorbed practitioners set us all back by confusing the public and raising skepticism among critics. It's better to admit failure or come up with information the client might not want to hear than to lie or exaggerate one's ability.

But, again, how will you know? Let's say you're at a psychic fair and you know nothing about the participating psychics. A few of them offer just what you're looking for. You even click on a personal basis with one or two. That's all well and good. But you shouldn't choose on that basis alone. After all, you're not there to make friends (some of the best fakes are as warm and charming as can be; it's all part of their shtick). Remember what I said about intuition and common sense? Ask yourself: Is this person a little too enthusiastic to take my money? Do the things this person says seem too good to be true? Does this person operate in a way that feels legitimate? Then start asking the sensitive some questions, and don't feel like you're being rude doing it—a legitimate sensitive won't feel offended at all. In fact, they'll welcome your skepticism because it means you're looking for truth, not entertainment.

Here are some suggestions on what to ask and what to look for:

Have you been tested? You want to know if they have been vetted by someone who knows what they're doing, someone who deals with psychics all the time (in my estimation, about three-quarters of psychics at psychic fairs have never been tested). If they tell you their Uncle Harry can verify their skills, that's not good enough. Ask if they belong to any group that you can't even get into without proving your ability. For example, some online groups like California Psychics won't allow a sensitive to be on its panel without first going through a rigorous vetting process. Psychic Sources and IN Psychic, as well as any program that cares about its reputation and its clients also do rigorous testing. A good psychic will be happy to give you their test results.

Do you have any documented feedback? If the psychic has a website, she's sure to have some testimonials. Ask for a list or else go to her website and see what people are saying. Pay particular attention to whether the feedback concerns the particular skill set you are looking for.

How do you proceed? And the related question, **what kinds of questions will you ask?** A psychic who asks too many questions is probably not as good as he claims—or not good at all. Some questions are necessary, of course, as the psychic needs to know what kind of reading you're after. But if you get the sense the psychic pumps for information he should already know, walk away. Also, when the reading starts, be careful not to give clues through your body language.

What's your fee? This is a no-brainer, but it should also be followed up by another question: **How does this fee**

compare to other psychics? If the psychic is expensive, it's a clue she's in it just for the money, and hence is not looking out for your interests. Today's psychics should not charge more than $150 an hour at the top end.

What does your fee cover? Let's say you met a psychic and told her about a problem you've been having. The psychic tells you, "You're suffering from a curse, I'm the only person who can get rid of it and I'll do it for $5,000." Aside from the fact you should be wondering why only *she* could remove it, you should be wondering why she wants so much money. Is it because the job is going to take an enormous amount of time? Or does she just think she's worth it? I'd walk away if I were you. Same with psychics who say they see a disease or disorder inside you, and can remove it, but only after getting a big fee. Walk away.

What's your address? A psychic with a post office box for an address is probably not reliable. She should be able to give you a physical address.

How long have you been reading? This is a no-brainer, too, but you'd be surprised how seldom it gets asked. If she's been at it a long time, she should have some kind of media coverage to show you, such as feature articles and YouTube videos. She might also have some documentation of success. I know this isn't like other services where it's easier to document success, but a good psychic should at least have some street cred and a few stats to back it.

Most of all use common sense—and your intuition. You don't have to be a sensitive to have intuition. We all pick up subtle clues about a person the first time we meet them. Our mind processes this information, often without us even being aware of it. This is why we sometimes get a bad feeling about someone we just met without really knowing why, only to find out later that we were right. Trust yourself.

13.

Dos and Don'ts

An insincere and evil friend is more to be feared than a wild beast; a wild beast may wound your body, but an evil friend will wound your mind. -- Dalai Lama

Before I get into the final lesson of this book—how to reach out to higher realms—I want to first go over some important do's and don'ts. Just as initial exploration of the physical realm has its dangers, so does exploration of the spirit realm, and I want to be sure you understand what those dangers are and how to avoid them.

As a matter of fact, I believe *every* book on self-help should include a cautionary note to its readers. You find warning labels on all sorts of products, from handheld blow dryers (don't use it in the bathtub) to cars (keep small children out of the front seat). Even when it seems the warning is superfluous since common sense should dictate anyway, it's not a bad idea to be reminded that danger is inherent in almost any product, or even action.

As to the latter, how many times do you hear of a family dying in a house fire because their smoke detectors weren't working properly? It happens, and it could have been prevented had they only checked the detector by pushing that little red button once in a while to see if the thing beeps. Yet how many of us don't even think about doing that? The same is true if you don't plan ahead and know what you're getting into. For example, every late spring or early autumn hikers get into trouble in high mountain ranges. It's a warm day at the bottom, but when they get up higher the weather turns colder. Maybe it starts to rain and they didn't bring a jacket or rain gear. Soon hypothermia is setting in and they're fighting for their life.

Preparation and awareness are important to any endeavor, and the realm of the psychological and spiritual is no different. So here's a list of things you should understand, and act accordingly:

Don't go it alone. Whenever possible, work with a group or at least a proven sensitive who knows what they're doing. This is especially important for those who wish to contact the spirit world, whether they're ghost-hunting or testing their mediumship. When first starting out, it's possible to naively mistake a deceptive demon for a benign spirit. A demon—even a bad human-spirit—might try to take advantage of an unsuspecting newbie. This potential problem will go away in time, but it's best to be cautious when you're first starting out.

Another reason to work with others is the learning curve. I find that you can learn much faster when working with others. There is so much knowledge and experience to exchange, just like in a classroom setting. Yet be alert to, and definitely avoid, any groupthink mentality you encounter. By groupthink I mean the temptation to please your peers by agreeing with their agenda. Independent thinking is a must for anyone trying to find her path to higher energy. Which brings me to my next pointer.

Don't follow advice blindly. Here I'm talking about more than groupthink; I'm speaking about independent action as well as thought. I find that a lot of professional psychics tend to teach strict methods that have worked for them, thereby imparting their own way of doing things on their students. But everyone is different, and I'm a firm believer that we all must do what works for us individually.

That's not to say you shouldn't try your teacher's methods, provided you trust her. However, if her specific advice isn't working it might be that something else works for you. Don't think, "Oh boy, I'm doing this all wrong and

I'm going to screw it up." Did you every notice that every major league pitcher has his own, unique windup and delivery? They were taught early on to draw back their leg and kick then push off the back leg while delivering with the arm. Yet some pitchers draw back higher or farther behind the back. And their delivery can be anywhere from over the shoulder to sidearm or even submarine style. Each has found his own way of throwing—unique mechanics that feel right to him—yet all pitchers start with the same method taught since grade school: draw back, kick, push off with the back leg, deliver.

So take what you are taught and learn it well, but don't be afraid to tweak it in whatever way works best for you.

Don't forget your goal. People often come to me seeking "something," yet they don't really know what that something is. Maybe enlightenment, maybe peace, maybe an answer to a burning question. They're really not sure. If they hadn't come to me they most likely would have looked for a way to contact the spirit realm without really understanding what they were doing. Often they think any contact is good contact because it confirms life beyond this earthly realm. A noble idea, but in every other way a bad one.

Why? Well, let me ask you this: would you wander through a city looking for something without knowing the neighborhoods? You might find yourself on the wrong side of the tracks being confronted by some bad guys. There are bad guys out there in the spirit world, too. Know who or what you want to contact ahead of time. Don't just fling open the door and see what wanders in; you can't always trust who or what is coming through. This is why spirit boards such as the popular Ouija are so dangerous. A spirit board works like an open portal that anything can come through, and dark spirits and demons take advantage of that. You might think you're asking questions of a departed loved one, but it might in fact be a demon trying to fool you. I don't recommend spirit boards of any kind, even the seemingly innocuous ones sold at toy stores. Which brings me to my next pointer.

Don't treat this as a game. Contacting the spirit world is not a game any more than making crank phone calls. Spirits—especially those that once existed in the flesh—want respect as much as living beings. Moreover, they're still here because they haven't been able to cross over to the realm where they really belong, which might frustrate them. I cringe every time I hear of so-called ghost hunters entering a haunted site and calling out stupid questions or even saying mean things just to entice a spirit to communicate. This is never a good idea. If you disrespect spirits they will likely ignore you, or worse, retaliate. I've heard stories of ghosts following ghost hunters home and wreaking havoc with their lives.

Remember this: if you respect the spirit world, it will respect you back. Even demonic forces, but for different reasons. Demons are nothing more than dark spirits that never existed in the flesh, and they have nothing but bad intent. They're also quite clever. They love to lie and deceive and turn your mind. And, yes, they will possess humans if given the chance. Yet what people don't really understand is that we humans have ultimate control when it comes to these entities. You see demons are like the schoolyard bully. If you show them that you're not afraid, *and* that you're protected, they won't bother with you. They have most of their success with the gullible and the weak; they know these types are easy targets for deception or intimidation. This is why they often target innocent children, addicts and the mentally infirm. But they'll stay away if they know their mind games won't work on you. Be prepared and they shouldn't bother you.

Do pray before you start. You may have seen ghost hunters on television saying a prayer before they start their investigation. This is smart. It doesn't mean you have to belong to any particular religion; in fact, your prayer doesn't have to follow any particular design. You can make up your own. It's all about asking a higher realm to be aware of your position and protect you. If you went hiking in the backcountry you would probably tell your family and friends where you were going in case something went wrong, wouldn't you? Even more, you might ask a buddy to come along in case you ran into trouble. When you pray, you are making sure all the energy stays positive as you step into another realm. Any negative entities lose their power when you call them out. Any positive entities will welcome you, knowing your intentions are good.

Do be spiritual. The spirit world likes to feel you are one with them when you visit. Moreover, Spirit likes to know you believe, as well as what follows from belief: acceptance. Without acceptance you aren't going to get very far anyway, because your mind and even your soul will be blocked from progressing. If you don't believe there's a rare bird hiding in those bushes, you'll never look hard enough to see it, right?

Do be cautious around pre-owned objects. It might sound unfair to all you yard sale enthusiasts, but I'm not being as harsh as you think. Everybody buys a used car at some time or another, or inherits furniture, paintings, pictures or other objects. That's fine. I'm talking about being cautious around something you don't know much about. More important, something that doesn't *feel right*. I can't tell you how many times I've wandered through an antique shop or auctioneer's house and suddenly felt uneasy as I came upon a particular object. It might be a portrait of a long-deceased person, but it can be almost anything that was owned before. There's a show called *The Haunted Collector* where the gentleman seeks out and takes away something in someone's house because the thing is haunted. It can be almost anything. He's legitimate, and his work is important. In fact, I have a couple of haunted paintings hanging in my own house. I took them away because they caused trouble for someone else. However, the entities haunting them have never bothered me because they know that 1) I respect them, and 2) I won't put up with any nonsense.

What does this mean? It means that not only buildings and graveyards can be haunted. The spirit of a dead person can attach itself to an object that once meant something to it, and for the same reason it might haunt a place: it feels familiar. The thing might be the only thing remaining in the physical world that makes sense or brings comfort. Thus a child spirit might cling to a teddy bear it loved, or a violent spirit might cling to the pistol it used for killing others.

So be aware of this fact, but don't obsess. If that old Tiffany lamp is calling to you, and it feels pleasant, it's probably okay to own it. But if you get the heebie-jeebies when you look at that antique beveled mirror, maybe you should pass on it.

Do be aware. Stay alert to what's around you. Be aware of how you feel, what you're thinking and so forth. This is a good practice anyway, right? Being aware means keeping your internal antenna up and activated at all times. Things are happening around you all the time, and not just physical things. You're always picking up information. That information is translated into feelings, thoughts and perceptions. When you drive by a building it might evoke something. When you meet a person for the first time he may remind you of someone else or even another time.

Pay attention to your dreams, too. Ever since Freud, dreams have been a favorite proving ground for psychologists. They love to interpret them, and you should, too. But don't get bogged down too much. Dreams usually happen because we're receiving information from our subconscious. It's trying out a new feeling or processing some information that came through that day in the earthly world. Yet sometimes information from another realm will find its way into a dream. Someone who crossed over might be trying to tell you something. For example, you might have a fleeting dream about your deceased grandmother catching you stealing cookies from the cookie jar as a child. Maybe this is her way of telling you that you've been eating too much, or eating the wrong kinds of foods and she's worried about your health. Similarly, in a dream your mom might be driving you in her old minivan, and you feel safe and small, like a child. This might be her spirit's way of letting you know she's nearby, watching over you.

The message might even be coming from a higher realm. People report about premonitions all the time. Sometimes the spirit realm brought those premonitions to us. Not human-spirits, but pure-spirits, which have access to such information. I've known people who had a certain premonition over and over for years and couldn't understand what it meant. Then one day the premonition came true, and it made perfect sense. Sometimes they were able to avoid bodily injury because they recognized an impending disaster through that premonition. Other times it only prepared them mentally and emotionally for something they were helpless to stop. Keep in mind that Spirit isn't about interfering with future events; it just wants us to be aware on some level.

As you develop your skills, you will probably add to the above list. It's part of that individuality thing I spoke of a few paragraphs back. But this list will serve you well as a starter kit. A toolbox you can add to later. Follow it earnestly and you can't go wrong.

14.

Onward, Outward, Upward

Progressive mental development means, in effect, extension of consciousness. – Carl Jung

A couple of chapters back I talked about awareness as the first step toward higher consciousness. Lao Tzu, author of the Tao Te Ching and one of the wisest humans ever to grace the earth, understood that higher consciousness begins with higher awareness. You see we are all capable of knowing and sensing so much more, yet most of us spend our brainpower focusing on more mundane things. It's like owning a super powerful computer, but using it for only one application—say, email or gaming—when there are so many other things it can do. Our brains are capable of awareness most of us can't even imagine, if only we learn the program!

In previous chapters I talked about balance and energy. Now I want you to learn how to become fully aware, and then tap into energy in ways you never have before. Once you've mastered this, you will understand better what I mean by balance and you will live a more balanced life. I should make clear up front that my aim isn't to make you a clairvoyant or a medium. However, in the course of your journey, don't be surprised if you gain knowledge and perspective you never dreamed possible.

So let's get started!

First find a comfortable, quiet place, one without any distractions. Perhaps a favorite room in your house, or a place outside where the only noise is the soft sounds of nature. Feel free to put on some quiet music, but only if it has no lyrical singing, as the words may distract you. Make sure the temperature is pleasant, and wear some loose, comfortable clothing. I recommend you sit on a comfortable piece of furniture, or a pillow if you choose the floor, as you could be in this position for an hour or more.

Now let's put to work what you've learned so far.

Meditation for higher consciousness is all about awareness, trust and acknowledgement. But it all begins with awareness. You'll recall our awareness exercise from Chapter 11, where you paid close attention to your physical environment. This time you will pay attention to what is presented to you outside the physical realm. Start by acknowledging that, as a human, you are part of a very special realm, one where the physical and spiritual are one. You are made up of atoms, molecules, cells, and chemicals—all physical things. The rug or chair or grass on which you are now seated is made of physical material, too. Yet each and every physical thing you see and feel can be converted to energy, energy so vast it can affect the universe itself. Acknowledge that energy. Accept it. Respect it.

Now acknowledge the non-physical part of you. This is what we call the soul, a spirit-like entity that can—and will at some point—exist apart from your physical body. Envision your soul in any form that makes sense to you. It doesn't matter if you see it as a misty sheet of energy, or an exact but ghostly replica of your physical self. The soul can be sensed as anything you want. Just be aware that your soul is not physical and it has an ability to commune with the universe in ways your physical self cannot.

Next, I want you to try acknowledging the entire universe. All of it, from the smallest of physical things to the largest—a grain of sand, perhaps, then a tree, then a vast ocean, and then the moon and planets and finally the stars and galaxies. Note that nothing can exist without everything else: a star, for example, must have atoms of the same elements, such as hydrogen and helium, found on planets, including our own. Physical things share some of the same elements with other, very different physical things. Thus all physical things are related, even if at a molecular level only.

And that includes you. You are related to everything—every planet, every star, every galaxy—in the universe.

The same is true of your soul. It may not have a physical makeup, but it has its own energy. The entire universe is filled with this same energy; thus you are connected to all things spiritually. More important, you have the ability to commune with all things without ever coming in physical contact with them.

Be aware of this. Acknowledge it. Now you are ready for the next step.

Close your eyes. Breathe evenly. Relax your muscles. Now, envision an orange. It's natural, it's bright, it's sweet. It nourishes the physical body in many ways. This orange floats before your inner sight. It will be there when you get back from your journey. Acknowledge this fact and find peace and comfort in it.

Now I want you to think about all of your troubles. Your problems, your cares, your doubts. Everything negative in your life, everything that causes you stress and negativity. Envision a sphere that you hold in your hands. It is empty now, but you're going to take each of your troubles and drop them one by one into the ball. It doesn't matter how big or how many, they will all fit. When you have emptied everything negative that clouds your mind, close the top of the ball. Do not discard the ball. Hold it in your hands as you journey.

That journey begins on a lower plane, a realm where you first leave your physical body behind. In your mind, envision a place that has no up or down or sides. There is no ceiling, neither is there a sky. No earth or floor. It is filled with fog, a fog in which you float. This is a realm without doubt, a realm where you will learn to trust whatever you encounter. As you float in the fog, wait and see what comes to you. Perhaps there will be nothing—it's not unusual for beginners to encounter nothing at first. However, if you do encounter anything, acknowledge it. It may be vague at first, but as you go through this exercise in the future it will get stronger. The important thing is to acknowledge and trust it.

Now you see the fog lifting. Light slowly filters through the parting mist, until it lifts away entirely and you find yourself floating in a place filled with white light. This is a realm of energy. Acknowledge how good the light feels, as it energizes your soul, pouring into the parts where it is needed. Allow the energy to go on flowing where it will. Trust it to find where it is needed most. Acknowledge it. Accept it. Enjoy its warmth and uplifting quality.

The light feels so good, so warm. But there soon comes a time when you need to cool down, to regulate your temperature. The light dims enough to see a new realm— the realm of perfect comfort. Here, the colors are green and aquamarine. The colors fall as drops onto your soul, cooling it, bringing it to the perfect temperature. Your energized soul begins to relax. It is soothed by the droplets and by the colors that surround you.

Once you are refreshed, see the colors give way to a place that reminds you of the Garden of Eden. Here, all things are good. The colors are a vibrant green. Everything is alive and healthy. The food and drink are perfectly nurturing. All things that you encounter—human or animal or spirit—communicate telepathically. They are at peace, and they want you to be, too. And so you are at peace, feeling you are as one with everything here and within the universe as a whole. Acknowledge this and accept it.

Soon you see two great pillars in the distance. You move toward them and find yourself outside a great hall. You walk through those pillars into that hall. This place is a library, but instead of books it is filled with spiritual files. All the knowledge of the universe is contained in here. There are other souls around the hall as well. They acknowledge you, as do the higher spirits that attend to the files. These are spirit teachers, saints and angels. They are all enlightened; they understand all things, and so they understand your soul. This time around they will most likely acknowledge you and nothing more, but in the future they will communicate with you as well. Acknowledge them and accept them.

Now you see a great doorway. It leads to another room. Walk through it and observe that the floor is a giant golden record. Surrounding it is a great judges' bench, and behind the bench sit spirits dressed in cloaks. Each one wears a different color. You are there to state your case to them, to unburden yourself of your worries and grievances. Take the ball you've been carrying and set it at the center of the floor. It will become a part of this golden record, which contains all of humanity's troubles since the beginning of time. Leave it there. You will not be taking it back with you. It is there for the spirits to take and examine. All of these concerns are now theirs. They no longer burden you. They are in the care of the spirits. *You* are in their care. Acknowledge these spirits and what they do, and be grateful. If the spirits wish to communicate, they will. If not, you needn't remain. Your task is done; you are now ready to return. Envision the orange again. It comes to you, growing in size, until it fills your vision. It is perfect in its shape and color and smell. It informs all your senses as you return to your physical body.

Slowly open your eyes. You needn't move yet. Bask in the good energy you've brought back with you. Enjoy the peace you feel after unburdening yourself. Rejoice in your first contact with the spirit realm. Think about what you saw and did. You can return any time you feel the need.

Meanwhile, know that your life has changed. If you followed the exercises in this book with trust and concentration, you will have begun a journey toward enlightenment and balance that no other method can duplicate or surpass. Your awareness will now be uplifted and made sharper. You will know how to find peace within yourself, instead of always trying to find it from without.

One more thing you will want to know: there is another realm, one for which you are not yet prepared. You see this realm is much closer to the Creator. It's a place where all the lessons you have learned are put in front of you, so you have to do the work first. You cannot see the place—you can't even reach it—until you've done the work. And this work takes time. Once you are prepared, you will understand that no human energy is involved, only spiritual. It's a realm of frequencies, light and energy, and it's eternal. Some people try to reach this realm too early, and they're always unsuccessful, as they should be. Such a prize doesn't come fast and easy.

We'll talk about this realm—and many other things—in a future book. For now, you need only rejoice in the fact that you've taken the first step on a path from which there is no return. You've opened a door that can't be closed—one you will never *want* to close. For you can't help but be more enlightened from here on. What's more, you have a tool that will bring you beyond mere meditation to greater enlightenment. Whenever life has you down, the exercises you've learned in this chapter will help. But overall, you are now going to understand one truth we all tend to forget, and that is that life is but one aspect of us. The rest is spiritual and eternal, and it exists within a universe of love and comfort. Be aware of this. Acknowledge it. Accept it.

You are on your way. Onward. Outward. Upward.

15.

A Final Word

Ask and it will be given to you; search, and you will find; knock, and the door will be opened for you. – Jesus Christ

Life is a journey. From beginning to end we pass through stages. Some we create for ourselves—rites of passage meant to acknowledge and celebrate these stages. Religious rites, graduations, wedding celebrations and so forth. Others come and go with barely an observation, but they're just as important. They're part of the natural progression of human life.

The preceding pages have been about the stages of human spiritual life. We sometimes forget that spirituality informs our mortal existence. From the time we are born to the moment we die we are driven by spiritual need and progress. It's no surprise that we humans crave spiritual

160

nourishment. It's hardwired into us because it's supposed to be. It's with us by design, not just mere evolution. There's a distinct purpose in being created in the flesh, rather than as spirit only.

What purpose is this? To put it succinctly, our physical selves exist for our spiritual side and not the other way around. Physical life is meant for experience. Experience leads to knowledge, and ultimately, wisdom. Everything we do in the flesh contributes to our individual experience. We humans are at a unique moment in progress. Yes, there are others in the universe (as we will soon know better) with a physical purpose as well, but they are not exactly like us. I believe this is because they have either not evolved as far as we have, or else surpassed us a long time ago. Speaking in evolutionary terms, we humans are in the midst of what might be described as a great and wonderful field trip designed to help us understand physicality in all its aspects. This knowledge will help round out our spiritual progress when we move on to a complete spiritual realm.

If you believe that the stars and planets and all the other matter existing in our universe has a purpose, then you are halfway to understanding what I'm talking about. The universe could just as easily have formed as empty space, or not formed at all. Instead, it exists as a duality of energy and matter, one related to the other. You could say one cannot exist without the other. You can even say that one *is* the other.

We humans happen to be both states contained in one package, and what a wonderful thing this is! As physical beings we have been able to progress from our ancestors' limited state to where we are today. As spiritual beings— our energy side—we have benefitted from that (seemingly) slow evolution, and are just now reaching a time of acceleration.

Think about it. For several millennia we laid the groundwork for this progression without even realizing it. Yet if you look back on just the past few hundred years, our craving for understanding of the cosmos and the spiritual world became so strong that it brought us to the next logical and natural step. That step is communion with the universe beyond our terrestrial home. I'm not talking about just physical space travel, for that can only bring limited knowledge and understanding. I'm also talking about another new frontier, which is communion through the human spirit. Communion while we are still in flesh form.

A couple of centuries ago space travel was considered a fantasy. Spiritual communion was thought of the same way, at least in Western culture. We took the first baby steps toward space travel in just the past hundred years. And those of us who wisely focus on our immortal soul and understand its connection to all other things are now taking baby steps toward greater enlightenment.

The purpose of this book has been to get you to take that first step yourself. I hope it has encouraged you to do that, and to take many more steps. If it has, then I've succeeded in my mission. That mission is to set each and every one of you free of your limitations. Limitations that cause your soul to be uncomfortable. But keep in mind that this book is only the equivalent of a first grade primer, a mere introduction to a new existence. It's up to each and every one of you to keep on following its lessons and to learn more, so you can continue your spiritual progress.

I, and others, will be there for you if you still need a teacher. Yet, like any good and caring teacher, I hope to one day hear my students tell me how much better their life is now that they have acknowledged and accepted what they are and what they can achieve.

Godspeed to all of you.

.

Printed in Great Britain
by Amazon

83617691R00102